1001, 2

Death's Other Kingdom

Death's Other Kingdom

A Spanish Village on the Eve of the Civil War

GAMEL WOOLSEY

With an afterword by Michael Jacobs

ELAND
London

First published by Longmans, Green and Co. in 1939

This edition published by Eland Publishing Ltd
61 Exmouth Market, London EC1R 4QL in 2004

ISBN 978 0 907871 19 4

Cover designed by Robert Dalrymple
Cover image © Serrania de Ronda, Spain, 1998
(oil on canvas), Fiona Bell-Currie (Contemporay Artist) /
Private Collection / The Bridgeman Art Library
Photographs on pages 11, 77, 147 and 153
© Lynda Pranger
Map © Reginald Piggott

Text set by Antony Gray
Printed in Spain by GraphyCems

To My Mother B. G. W.

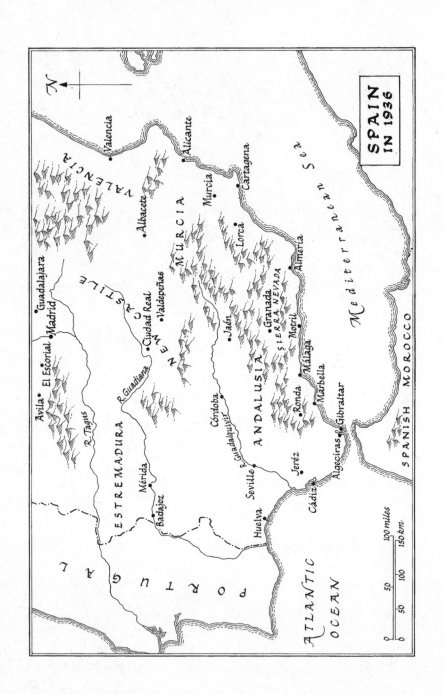

Chapter 1

IT WAS THE MOST BEAUTIFUL DAY of the summer – in all the rummage box of time there could hardly have been found a more beautiful day. The sky at dawn was cloudless and the 'pink band' of the tropics, the band of rosy light which ascends the sky from the horizon at twilight, rose to the zenith and faded into the growing light. Then the sun rose suddenly with a leap into the air: the long hot southern day had begun.

Enrique, our gardener, was already at work irrigating the tomatoes. As soon as the disc of the sun appeared, he stooped to tie up a straying tomato plant and went to shut off the water at the cistern. Then, without a moment's rest, he began to dig up the caked earth around the roots of the rose bushes; for the garden was his pride and his joy.

'*Va a hacer calor hoy!*' he said, wiping his forehead. 'Today it's going to be hot!' I saw him still working as I stood in my bathing-suit looking down from the landing, too late as usual to bathe in the cistern, for Enrique always would irrigate before dawn – he said the morning sun burned the wet leaves. So we could only take a shower-bath in the fountain, deliciously cold and shivery under the thin spray of cold water from the sierra.

I always loved waking in Spain. The sun fell in stripes from the slatted shutters on to the red and white diamonded tiles of the floor. Noises from the street below floated up; the pattering feet of the milk goats sounded like rain drops, and their plaintive Maaaaaaaaa trembled up, while they were being milked into our milk cans. A melancholy call

'*Pescao – de – lo – bueno –*' came up from the fish sellers, their hampers full of fresh fish just coming up from the sea on their lean donkeys. Another came crying the inevitable '*Hay sardinas – y – boqueronis –*' the food of the poor, the cheapest of fishes.

More street cries '*Hay uvas frescas y gordas –* ' 'grapes fresh and plump – '. '*Tomates y pimientos gordos –*' 'tomatoes and big pimentos'. Melons, lettuces, plums, squashes, peaches and pumpkins were passing, a perfect harvest festival going by on donkeys. All the delicious fruits of the rich *vega* of Malaga. From time to time we could hear Maria, our cook-housekeeper, bargaining, raising her voice in horror because melons were a farthing more today. But really we hardly bought anything in the way of fruit or vegetables, for Enrique's pride was to produce more of everything than we could possibly eat and give the superabundance to our neighbours who had no gardens.

We ate breakfast as usual in the garden by the fountain. The late summer flowers were ablaze, enormous dahlias like bursting rockets, and beds of zinnias in all the colours of a pastel rainbow, and twice as big as English ones, beds of odd crimson cockscombs, beds of everlastings, beds of brown and yellow daisies, big sunflowers against the garden wall. They were all rich warm colours, all overblowing as if ripe for a harvest of flowers. Far away we could hear the sound of mules galloping around the threshing floor over a carpet of golden corn: later in the evening when the *levante* rose they would winnow the grain with winnowing fans.

That day lunch was rather a fiesta for we had little red salmonetes, the most delicious of all the Mediterranean fish, but *very* dear – Maria groaned for they cost eightpence a pound. After these came the freshest of lettuces just picked in the garden and Enrique's ripe red tomatoes. There was the wine of the country, a very good white wine, and the marvellous Spanish country bread, firm in texture and tasting of ripe wheat; and of course to end with great bowls of fruit, grapes and peaches and melons. I do not know why I should remember this so well except that it was the last day we ever had like that.

The heat in the afternoon was intense, but it was a lovely wide sunny heat spread from horizon to horizon under the blue cloudless sky. We had no one staying with us, and it was nice to be alone again, for we had had visitors all spring. So many of our friends had come out to see our newly bought farmhouse where we hoped to live cheaply and at peace on the produce of our own gardens and orchards, far from the troubles of Europe in this remote Iberia where nothing ever changed.

It was lovely to have nothing in the world to do, and simply bask in the day like lizards in the shade of the high white garden wall. The house itself was a rough two-story farmhouse, probably very old. The walls were four feet thick, built of stone and rubble and plastered outside and in. They insulated us from heat in the summer – I cannot say from cold in the winter, for the pure white walls (with occasional splashes of bright colour from old glass pictures of the saints, and shelves of old Spanish pottery) and the smooth diamond tiles under foot, looked and were singularly chilly on a wet dark day in winter. Then the only warm place was the inside of a huge old fireplace in which we sat. But in hot weather nothing is so lovely as a big Andalucian house, gay with bright flowers, fresh, immaculate and cool in any weather.

Before tea that day we bathed in the irrigation cistern which had filled again: it was just long enough for four strokes, and the fresh mountain water always running was cold and crystal clear. We looked at the sea as we stood on the balcony after dressing and longed to be swimming in it, but it was much too far away to walk to in such heat, though the Mediterranean looked more lovely, more classical than ever. It was blue and still as a lake, and along the shore with its lace edging of foam the little fishing boats were sailing home, distant tiny white-sailed butterfly boats, sailing through this still fixed classical beauty – Ulysses returning – the Argonauts sailing home with the golden fleece.

We sat in the patio for tea by the fountain in the shade of the house. As we sat drinking our tea, but eating nothing, for food and tea never seem to go together in Spain in summer, the servants gathered round and stood leaning on the fountain and the cistern talking to us like retainers in a Shakespearian play. As they arrived we asked them to join us in eating '*Quieren ustedes comer?*' '*Gracias, que se sientan bien.*' They politely refused. 'Thank you, may it do you good,' with the beautiful manners of Spain where even a beggar by the road eating dry bread offers it courteously to the rich passer-by and is as courteously refused.

'Is there any news?' we asked Enrique, who had been to visit a gardener friend. 'Very little,' he said. 'The workers in the Oxide of Iron factory who struck and got twelve pesetas a day last month, are now striking for fifteen. It is too much – who can pay fifteen pesetas a day!'

It was a fabulous sum to Enrique who had earned three pesetas a day in the Alpujarras when he was lucky enough to be working at all, and now lived comfortably and put by money on the 120 pesetas a month he got from us. Of course he had his cottage and his electric light free, and all the vegetables and fruit he could eat from the garden.

He was twenty-five and still a bachelor – Maria our cook-house-keeper was his mother and lived with him in the gardener's cottage. Her daughter Pilar, a melancholy widow, lived in our house with her ugly little girl and did most of the work. Gerald, my husband, had brought them from the Alpujarras and they were devoted to him. Maria's father had been gardener to an uncle of his who had a house in the Sierra Nevada back of Granada where we had often stayed with him. And in their eyes we were all practically Granadinos together, a great bond between us in this foreign country of Malaga. For a village in Spain is a unity; its inhabitants are like members of a clan, they have a close and indissoluble bond. 'My village' is constantly in the mouth of a Spanish countryman. It is more than 'my country'.

The house at Churriana in 1935

Maria was tall and rather thin and still handsome at fifty-four, which is old for a Spanish woman. Her thick hair was still black and her smooth olive skin tightly drawn over the strong bones of the face. She always wore a black silk handkerchief over her hair and was always dressed in black. I suppose it had originally been mourning for her husband 'dead and in glory' for twenty years, but now like all old countrywomen of the ancient school in Spain, she always wore it as the only suitable wear for this woeful world.

She was rather a severe character, rather an old Roman. Devoted to our interests and very indulgent to our oddities after her fashion, she was hard upon mankind in general and spent a great deal of time in disapproving. *Novedad* – Novelty was her horror. Anything new was suspect. She would not have had a leaf change. And she spoke of *novedad* with the same intense disapproval as an old lady in the south whom I once, as a little girl, heard hold forth on a new electric tram service which was taking the place of the old mule-drawn cars. 'I have

11

no use,' she said, 'for these newfangled Northern ideas.' Maria ought to have been in her service.

Enrique, her son, was a very different character. He was a gentle, charming young man and loved flowers like a Linnaeus. He had hardly ever seen garden flowers except in pots in his native village in the Sierra Nevada, and our garden and orchard looked to him like the Garden of Eden. You could see him standing sometimes when he was not at work gazing up into a flowering orange tree with a sort of ecstatic wonder on his face as if he were waking in the morning of the world. The Spanish love of the land is far stronger even than that of the French, and to keep them from the soil by not cultivating the big estates and the waste land of Spain is like starving them amidst plenty.

Pilar, Maria's daughter, was a rather wan widow with one ugly little four-year-old daughter. Her life had been sad. She had married a poor labourer, a 'foreigner' from another village who had been a bad lot, ill-treated her, got into trouble and deserted her. Finally she had heard that he was dead. She had had to live with Maria and at Maria's expense, and until we bought our Malaga house and brought them all down with us to this land of plenty, they had suffered often from hunger and cold in their high mountain village. Maria had disapproved of the marriage and blamed Pilar for the outcome, and treated her severely, though like all Spaniards she loved children too much to be anything but kind and indulgent to her little grand-daughter, the result of it. But Pilar's sad, patient face, which seemed ready to silently endure hunger, cold and privations of every kind, always seemed to me like an illustration for the life of the Spanish poor. Without being beautiful in any usual sense of the word, it had its own bleak austere beauty, like the beauty of some austere Spanish landscapes, where the grey granite and the yellow earth mount with bare unbroken noble lines to the sky without a tree, or, one would have said, a flower, and yet the grey fragrant herbs clinging to the barren slopes feed great flocks of goats that pass with all their bells ringing, and myriads of bees droning through the bright day.

That afternoon Pilar was leaning, as she often did, on the back of my chair as we talked. This position, affectionate and familiar and also claiming protection, seemed always to me very characteristic of the relations of Spanish servants and masters at their best. They were our 'family' in the old sense of the word, as when the disgraced Wolsey asks Henry to remember his 'family', his household retainers. And their relation to us was not one of monthly payments, of hiring and giving notice. We could as soon have given our own children notice. Pilar one day was scolding the poor little four-year-old. 'Don't scold her so hard for such a little thing,' I protested. 'I want to bring her up to do me credit when she is your servant,' Pilar said, 'not to be my shame.' The poor little Mariquilla was already appointed to serve my older years. And if we both live there is no doubt but that she will.

Tea was over, and the servants scattered to their various tasks. Enrique to stirring up the caked hot earth in the zinnia beds to give the roots air, and preparing for his evening irrigating, which he would not begin until after the sun had set, Maria to prepare the evening meal, a great *cazuela* of chicken, rice and all sorts of green vegetables, and onions, tomatoes and peppers all cooked together in a huge earthenware pot over a charcoal fire, and one of the most delicious meals imaginable. I saw Pilar and the little Mariquilla crossing the garden on their way to feed the chickens and rabbits, carrying bundles of alfalfa and a basket of maize and kitchen scraps. They were laughing over some childish joke, escaped for the moment from Maria's severe eye. Poor Pilar was wearing an old dress of mine which I had just given her, and which she had hurriedly altered to fit. Clothes were her one frivolity, and her timid pride was entirely set in them. She liked to go to the shops in the village wearing a new dress and nice leather shoes, but also wearing an apron to show that she was appearing in her role of servant in a big house of the English, and that if she were going to pay a visit, or to shop in Malaga, she could wear something much better. She had lately begun appearing in an old coat of mine, to my distress, leaving off the graceful peasant shawl.

A lovely little wind was blowing from the sea, and the 'pink band' was rising to the zenith; there it spreads, fades, and evening comes. We went out to the end of the garden and sat in a little *mirador* on top of the wall so that we could look out over the world beyond, over a lovely field of green maize already growing tall, to the olive yards stretching away towards the distant blue mountains. To our left rose grey, stony hills covered with grey herbs that fill the air with aromatic scents of rosemary, thyme and lavender wherever you walk on them. I could hear a sheep bell that seemed as if it came from a thousand miles away, it was so thin and far away sounding. The bats had come out and were flitting like black butterflies among the sharp-winged swallows which were performing their airy evening dance. The sky was yellow with soft diffused light pouring up from under the edge of the world.

Some labourers going home through the field called their friendly greeting. '*Buenas noches, Don Geraldo*,' '*Buenas noches, Señora!*' '*Vaya usted con Dios.*' 'Go with God,' we answered. Two young workmen came by after them. '*Salud!*' they called, the Popular Front greeting, '*Salud!*' Gerald answered rather half-heartedly, but I answered them too, 'Go with God.' '*Salud*' seemed curt and ugly after the soft '*Buenas noches*', and the splendid '*Vaya usted con Dios*'. Surely the most beautiful greeting in any language. And the young men's voices seemed to have an aggressive ring, and their harsh '*Salud*', though it was spoken with friendly smiles, seemed to break rudely through the lovely evening sights and sounds like an aggression from other worlds of factories, labour troubles and strikes. The evening was too lovely to be thinking of agrarian reforms and the doubtful future of Spain.

The first star had appeared and the scent of the huge night-smelling datura blossoms came drifting towards us; the little green flowers of the dama-de-noche were opening in the darkness and their lovely scent began to fill the air.

The sounds of the village came floating up to us, dogs barking, children playing, women calling; and the bitter-sweet scent of burning herbs mixed with the scent of flowers in the darkening air. The lovely day was over, the tranquil evening drew into a peaceful tender night.

Chapter 2

SOMEONE WAS SINGING 'London Bridge is Burning Down, Burning Down – ' They're getting it all wrong, I thought. 'It's falling down, isn't it? Or *is* it burning down?'

Then I started awake. Maria was standing at the foot of the bed. 'Why are you sleeping,' she said, 'when Malaga is burning down?'

We leapt out of bed asking 'What has happened? What is it?' still half asleep.

'There's been a rising,' she said, 'and they've set fire to the city.'

We rushed to the window.

Malaga lying spread out across the bay was under a pall of smoke. The city was hidden and the smoke drifted far out over the sea. Malaga is burning down.

'But what has happened?' we kept asking and no one could tell us. Lorries full of armed workmen began to appear, rushing down the road. As they passed they threw up their left arms in the Popular Front salute, the clenched left fist and bent arm. With the pistols in their right hands, loaded and cocked and ready to go off, they waved to us gaily.

'Someone will get killed soon,' said Enrique sardonically, 'and it won't be a Fascist, but one of us if we don't stay indoors.'

'*Salud!*' yelled a passing lorry with brandished fists and waving pistols. '*Salud!*' we yelled back. The lorries came thicker and faster, brandishing pistols, bristling with rifles, singing the 'Internationale'. They were chalked with the initials of all the Left parties, UGT Socialists, CNT Anarcho-Syndicalists, FAI the extreme Anarchists.

In the front of one lorry stood a young Anarchist like the figure-head of a ship. He held the Red and Black Flag clasped to his breast. His eyes had ceased to see the village street, the passing cars: they saw close to him, just ahead, the Future World! Man free and happy, man just and good, work for all, bread for all, love for all. In his dream he was leading us all to the future world. Man's Promised Land.

'*Salud! Salud!*' The lorries went thundering by. Where were they going? They knew as little as we did. The Revolution from the Right, thwarted in its inception, had given birth to the Revolution from the Left. Hope and promise were in the air – you could see that for them 'Bliss was it in that dawn to be alive.' And the lorries thundered by in a never ending stream. And the day went on, bright and hot, with hope and determination in the air.

What had happened, we kept on asking, and got various confused accounts. There had been a fight between some soldiers who tried to seize the Government buildings and the Guardias de Asalto and the soldiers had deserted their officers. Then in the early dawn the poor quarters rose and burnt a lot of houses, two hundred houses, four hundred houses. We ate our *cazuela* for supper and went to bed, but we could not sleep much. Lorries dashed by, lights glared in the windows, cries, shouts, grinding of brakes. *Salud! – Salud! –* the Revolution.

'*Salud!*', roaring engines, grinding brakes, a distant rifle shot. Daylight again. Has anyone slept? The same lorries are dashing by. Grimy but happy, the young men wave their pistols and throw up their clenched fists in a gesture of triumph. Malaga is in the hands of the workers. And the pale smoke still hangs like a pall and drifts far out to sea.

As we were eating breakfast a patrol arrived searching for arms. But they knew us and refused to search our house. The English, they said, were the friends of Spain. So we all had some *aguardiente* and they left. *Salud! Salud!* Later when Gerald had gone out to visit a friend, a second patrol arrived. They were strangers from Malaga and hammered on the big front door. I went down to receive them with the servants behind me and they came in with their guns held forward as if boarding a pirate. The young leader to my intense delight was armed with a child's toy gilt sword. I looked behind me, the servants to my surprise and displeasure had disappeared completely; so I showed the little band upstairs myself. They went into my bedroom, and the young leader opened a bureau drawer: it was unfortunately filled with my silk underclothes. Overcome with modesty he hurried from the scene of embarrassment leaving all the other drawers and chests unopened.

We went downstairs again and into the dining-room where the young leader with evident apprehension opened the drawer of an old table. It was full of headless dolls, the property of Pilar's little daughter. The young leader felt that Fate was mocking him, and his companions certainly were. The servants had reappeared, and ushered the patrol out, all but the leader on a broad grin. *Salud! Salud!*

'Where were you?' I asked the servants.

'Oh, we were just hiding the silver and your jewellery,' they said. The distrust of Spaniards for other Spaniards is bottomless and blinds them often to reality. I could see at a glance that the young leader with his toy sword was a fanatic of the purest water. The Koh-i-noor would not have tempted him while he was doing his duty. He might have killed me in the pursuit of Anarchy, but he would never have stolen from me. But I did not argue the point uselessly with the servants. All strange Spaniards from other towns were probably robbers to them. The innocent stupid English, they think, do not understand these things; and so are always robbed and cheated.

All that morning the lorries roared and thundered and hailed *Saluds* with undiminished zeal. In the afternoon our village friends, the carpenters and masons and gardeners began to visit us. There was a rumour, they came to warn us of it, that house burning was going to spread, a band of extremists from the city were said to be coming to burn down some local houses.

'They wouldn't burn ours?' we asked with some doubt.

'*Claro que no!*' they said surprised. The idea of anyone however fanatical burning the houses of the innocent and slightly ridiculous English had never entered their heads.

'But they'll burn your neighbour's house, old Don Cristober's. He is a Fascist. And with this wind it might catch your roof; but we'll stay and help. We'd better borrow buckets and have some brooms and some buckets of sand ready.' We were to be calmly prepared for what seemed to us all a natural catastrophe.

Gerald mourned a little. 'It's such a beautiful old house,' he said. 'Yes, it is a pity,' said Juan the carpenter with resignation. 'I do all their work and the wood is very good. It is a pity.' But cyclones and civil wars are all felt as 'acts of God', or acts of the devil – there is no use protesting against anything that happens in them.

Crowds of people were gathering in the street. Don Cristober's old gardener and his witchlike wife came to us to ask us if we could not do something to help them. Gerald told them when the house-burning party came they had better suggest their burning the furniture (which was awful anyway) and leaving the house, which might be used for a school or hospital. 'Then at least you'll save the house and also keep a roof over your own heads,' he said. Time passed and nothing happened, so we went up on the roof to look at Malaga – the smoke still streamed out from the town like a long woeful banner trailing out on the air to tell of disaster.

We were looking towards the distant sea when suddenly from a big white house not far away sprang up a thin white column of smoke – 'oh, Lord, it's come,' I thought with that sickening feeling of the worst arriving. The smoke got thicker and thicker, eddying in clouds – then a red flame appeared, then a great burst of flame and smoke, the roof had fallen in. Far away to the left a second column of smoke appeared.

We waited rather grimly, but no one came, nothing happened, no more fires appeared.

'Not a good day for burning houses,' said Gerald, making me laugh, for he sounded as if he were apologising for them. The thermometer stood at ninety-four degrees and it was breathless – 'so hot standing round a fire. Perhaps they'll come tonight. Fires are much finer at night anyway.' But that evening a sinister rumour began to run about the village, so sinister that everyone forgot all about burning houses.

'*El Tercio!*' '*El Tercio* is coming!' From the tone of the voices we heard in the street they might have been saying 'Hell has opened!' 'Lucifer and his legions are upon us!' For it was a Legion that was coming.

El Tercio (The Force) is the Foreign Legion, the only regular soldiers, except twelve thousand Moors, that Spain possessed. I do not know if they deserve the dread the people showed of them. But there were ugly tales of what they did at Oviedo. There were only six thousand of them, but they made up in courage and ferocity for their lack of numbers, and I have heard foreign soldiers say that they would take on the Prussian Guard or their own weight in wild cats.

This was the Legion worthy of Lucifer that was expected, and the expectation ran like a cold wave of horror through the countryside. No one went to bed. Everyone was abroad on the road watching the red flare of Malaga, listening if they could hear on the distant highway the tramp of the approaching enemy. And the whisper '*El Tercio, El Tercio*' ran from mouth to mouth in a tone of blood-curdling fear that communicated itself to us in spite of ourselves, chilling our blood, echoing fearfully in our unwilling ears.

We went at last to bed hearing the splutter and misfiring of a little aeroplane droning bravely off to blow up bridges and hinder the Legion's advance. The lorries were still rushing by – some to go towards Algeçiras carrying eager youths to defend their villages, some into the mountains to defend the passes against the 'Fascists', who had ceased already to be *Don Fulano* (Don Somebody-or-other) and his sons and nephews and cousins, and become a quite mythical figure of wickedness and horror rather like the figure of the 'Red' in the mind of a *Daily Mail* reader. Figures of fun, 'Hodadoddys' of the mind's cabbage garden, figures to laugh at if they were not used to frighten all reason out of the air.

The dark night was lit by the glow from Malaga, and the ruddy dark was suddenly punctured by the white flare of headlights rushing by. As I sank into a deeper darkness of sleep – I heard a voice below whisper *'El Tercio'* like the voice of fear itself.

Chapter 3

MORNING CAME, and nothing had happened after all. The Legion, they now said, was far away near Algeçiras. Everything was going to be all right. They would be kept there. The Moors, except the few that had crossed, would be kept in Africa. But there was a more sober look about things. There were more lorries on the road than ever, but they had a new determined air, as if they had something serious to do, somewhere important to go.

The kitchen was full of poor old countrywomen who had already begun to see Moors behind every bush and had come for protection and consolation. That day for the first time we flew our English flag. We had bought it at the Army and Navy Stores for just such occasions if they should eventuate. But we had not liked to put it up before because we had no Spanish flag to fly with it. But Pilar had hastily run one up out of odds and ends of old coloured dresses and we hung them both out on the balcony where they were received with enthusiasm by the passing lorries. And it was a great comfort to the servants and to all our poor neighbours, who said 'Now the house is sacred. No one can touch it.'

'Let's go to Torremolinos to see Gray and find out what has happened,' Gerald said.

Gray was an American friend, a journalist, who had taken a villa in Torremolinos, a village by the sea where there is a large English colony eked out with foreigners of other nationalities. Gray was trying to write a book on the confused subject of modern Spanish politics and so we felt that he ought to understand better than the rest of us what was really happening.

'It's dreadfully hot,' I said. There were no buses running and the very thought of those long dusty miles under this burning sky made me tired and thirsty.

'Never mind, some one will give us a drink and we can have a swim in the sea.' Maria unwillingly made us up a *merienda*, a picnic lunch. 'You'd much better stay at home in your own garden, and not go on the roads and get yourselves shot by these ill-educated youths,' she said severely, with the scorn of the true conservative Spaniard, hating all forms of *novedad*, distrusting all change either to left or right.

'*Vaya usted con Dios*,' she said disapprovingly as we went out of the kitchen door into the street. '*Salud!*' yelled a passing lorry load. '*Salud!*' we yelled back with an excitement we could not repress. '*Con Dios*,' said Maria so disapprovingly that it amounted to a curse, but her 'with God' was drowned in the hail of '*Saluds*'. And she went inside and shut the door with a bang.

We set off. Heavens, how hot it was! Not a breath from the sea, as we toiled down the seemingly endless way. Presently we left the tarred high road with relief and escaped the thundering lorries. As we climbed down the narrow yellow goat tracks our feet crunched the rosemary and thyme, and the sharp bitter-sweet scent rose in the hot air.

At last we could see Torremolinos, small and white on the edge of the sea. Exhausted by the heat we sat down in the shade of an olive tree and opened our lunch. It was a true Spanish *merienda*, cold potato omelette, a little goat's milk cheese, half a loaf of bread, early muscatels and a small bottle of white wine. The blue sea was as quiet as it had been three days before. An air of everlasting peace, of classical peace rising from the deep past brooded over the Mediterranean. But suddenly far off inland we heard a rattle of shots, and to the left the ominous smoke of Malaga burning was still drifting out to sea.

A little wind was springing up, a tiny but fresh *levante*. It blew in our faces as we continued on our way; a long hot pull through the level plain among crops of beet sugar. Two patrols stopped us, but when they realised that we were English they only saluted and laughed. 'These aren't Fascists,' they said grinning.

Torremolinos at last. Longing for coffee we stopped at the first café – locked and shut. 'All the cafés are shut,' said an onlooker. 'Order of the governor. No place that sells liquor is allowed to serve anyone with anything.'

Thirsty and weary, we turned down a street towards the sea and knocked at Gray's door. Our friend, who opened it, was a big dark American, 'Thank heavens, you're here. Do give us a drink, the cafés are shut. And tell us what has happened.'

'Hell's broken loose,' he said pulling out a bottle of white wine and some glasses from the cupboard. 'Maria,' he shouted to his old fat cook, '*Café para tres.*'

'Yes, but how did it begin?'

Generals in Morocco rose first. Everywhere in Spain they've tried to seize the Government buildings. Failed here completely, succeeded in Seville, and God knows where else. I don't suppose they can do much really unless they can get all the Foreign Legion and the Moors over. And I don't see how they can because the Government has got practically all the Navy. The officers rose, but the sailors refused to obey orders. Only one merchant ship brought over a boatload of Moors and Legionaries. Then the sailors seized the boat and took her off somewhere. The sailors on the warships have seized their officers and put them in chains or thrown them overboard, anyway they are all for the Government, or so people here say.'

Old Maria came in with the coffee just then.

'*Maria, como está usted en estos tiempos malos?*'

'*Malísimos están! y a estos locos que van por las calles en coches con revólveres se deben de ponerlos todos en la carcel.*' 'And these idiots who run about in motorcars with revolvers ought all to be in prison.' Maria was as unsympathetic as our Maria over the popular excitement.

Gray laughed, his tolerant, kindly, western laugh.

'She is a Fascist,' he said to Maria's indignation.

Fascist was already bandied about as a word of violent abuse. It had become the extreme of insult, even ousting *sinverguenza* from its place of honour.

Maria went out muttering about the evil of these times.

'What are Maria's politics?'

'Complete disapproval of anything that was not done in her time in her hometown, Cártama – complete loyalty to Cártama – mild dislike of all the rest of Spain, distrust of all "foreigners", that is to say all Spaniards not born in Cártama.'

'How can she bear living away from it then?'

'Well you know, she's like the Boston Irish. She loves Cártama even more from a distance. But you'll see that she'll go back. She stays with me because I pay her well and she's rather fond of me, and thinks these awful robbers of Torremolinos would fleece me if she weren't here to protect me. Ask her about her twelve olive trees in Cártama some time. They've all got names and personalities. One is "the one with the broken bough", another is "the one where they hung the fox". I'm sure she prays for them and I expect they come when they are called.'

We all drank Maria of Cártama's coffee. Delicious after the thirst and tiredness of that endless hot road.

'I'm off this afternoon,' Gray said.

'Where to?'

'To Morocco to see what's happening, or to Madrid if I can get there by plane, or to Seville. There's no use staying here. Malaga isn't likely to be important. I want to see some of this fuss before it's over. And you can't send news out from here anyway. Everything's censored.'

'But how'll you get away? There aren't any trains or buses and surely you can't pass the Rebel lines at La Linea, can you, even if you could get a car?'

'I shan't try. I've got a fishing-boat that's promised to take me. Goes to Gibraltar smuggling every night anyway. My local friends will help me hop a lorry to Fuengirola. Then the fishing-boat and Gibraltar at dawn if we have luck.'

'And a prison in Seville if you don't, I suppose,' said Gerald sardonically.

'Or a nice roomy grave in the Mediterranean. I don't believe the Rebels are up to catching us. But the worst of it is I'm a hell of a bad sailor. I shall be sick as a dog all night on that beastly fishy lugger. And I'll look and smell so horrid that your conservative fellow countrymen will throw me back when they see what they've caught.'

'Don't you want to pack?' Gerald asked.

'Oh, I'm packed already, I wanted to go this morning but there was no way. Stay till my friends come – God knows when we'll meet again. I shall go to America when I've had a look around. Spain's going to be a hell of a place to write books in for the next year or so.'

'I shouldn't try, too exciting just watching it.'

Someone knocked upon the door, and two young men in blue overalls came in. And we all greeted one another *Salud! Salud! Salud!*

'Hurry!' they said. Gray seized his typewriter and suitcase. Goodbye! Goodbye! Salud! Salud!

Maria of Cártama stood in the doorway dolefully shaking her head.

Wearily we walked home. The sun was going down, but walking was still a penance. Our Maria greeted us crossly. She was glad to see us safe home, but she felt that something *ought* to have happened to us. The Spanish have a proverb which she quoted to us that night. 'The foolhardy who get themselves killed are the Devil's martyrs.'

Chapter 4

I HAVE FORGOTTEN to mention that we were carrying a burden on our way back from Torremolinos which added to our discomfort in the dust and heat. Gray as he was leaving had urged us to take his radio so that we could get some news from outside, and we had decided to lug it with us lest it should be confiscated before we were able to come back for it. It was a horrid-looking little radio, but we were glad of its small proportions at the time as it was quite heavy enough as it was to carry for miles uphill; but later we discovered what a wretched little thing it was. Voices roared and bellowed and squeaked out of it, all languages sounded alike and all incomprehensible, every station seemed to talk at once on every wavelength, and yet it was almost impossible to find the particular station you wanted at all. When you finally got some English station, either Czechoslovakia was sending directly on top of it, or Seville or Malaga were buzzing on its wavelength to prevent you from getting any outside news. Yet, bad as it was, it became one of the greatest interests of our lives, and after six o'clock (when the electric light in the village was turned on) we were almost always to be found seated in front of its varnished face trying to get some meaning out of the chaotic sounds which strangely roared and shrieked out of it.

Radio in time of war becomes absolutely fascinating. The pronouncements, denials, alarms, rumours, propaganda, speeches of national leaders, make it enthralling to the listener who is at all emotionally involved, especially if he can follow the news in several languages. When we turned the hand on the little dial, harsh voices began to speak, excited, alarmed, denunciatory. After we had heard the news about Spain – the uncertain rumours rather – from England, France and Germany, we listened to Spain herself.

Malaga broadcast perpetually, and always at the top of her lungs. Voices cried on us to stand firm, to repel the wicked Fascists – they are beaten everywhere already, but we must stand firm and complete the victory, destroy them once for all. Then, work for man's good, create happiness everywhere, build a glorious new Spain. Other voices were issuing instructions, announcing meetings. Sometimes when even the brazen voices grew tired there was music, *cante hondo*. Madrid spoke more soberly, the crisis was great, but we would meet and overcome it, the voices said. Sometimes some famous politician made an address. Prieto did once, but he is not at all a good speaker, and while his remarks were sensible, no doubt, the only thing which I can remember was a joke he made. The worst thing about the rebellion, he said, had been the weather. The heat in Madrid was at its height, and Prieto, a large fat man with a million things to do was feeling it severely. Azaña only spoke once, at midnight; but it was a very fine speech, simple and from the heart.

A type of announcement which was a pathetic feature of all the Spanish broadcasts, Government and Insurgent alike, were those which individuals and families were allowed to make when they were separated from their relatives and friends and wanted to inform them of their safety. They were always in the same form: 'Juan Lopez of Malaga, now in Madrid, wants to inform his family that he is safe and *sin novedad*,' that is, that nothing has happened to him.

'The family of Maria Martín of Velez want to inform their relatives in Granada that they are safe and well.' But we seldom heard them, for they were given during the day when the stations were least busy, and when our radio was not working, so we only occasionally caught a few as we passed some café, whose radio going full blast was always surrounded by a crowd of silent listeners standing in the street within hearing distance.

But the thing we waited for most eagerly was not the foreign stations nor the Government's but the Insurgent broadcasts from Seville. During the day Seville played music and made personal announcements, in the evening the news began, and I might as well mention at this point that this news was far more accurate than news from the Government side, having indeed some relation to fact which Government news then never did, being simply a recital of triumphs and victories, almost all entirely imaginary, so that we listened anxiously to Seville hoping to get at least some faint idea of what was really going on in Spain. The BBC news at that time appeared to be obtained by adding together news from Madrid and Seville and dividing by three; it was always unlikely and generally fantastic sounding. The French was slightly more reliable, we always felt, perhaps only because the resonant voices of the French announcers carried more conviction than the mealy mouths of the BBC. But with this lack of any probable-sounding news from abroad it is easy to imagine with what excitement we turned on Seville every night hoping by a process of deduction, elimination and guess work to gather from what they chose to tell us at any rate some information about the rapidly changing state of affairs in the country.

Still it was not the news from Seville, however surprisingly related to truth, which made us wait for her broadcasts so eagerly every night, but the speeches of that amazing 'radio personality', General Queipo de Llano. Unfortunately few English people speak Spanish or listen in to Spanish stations; for it is very unsatisfactory to have to try to describe Queipo de Llano, he has to be heard. Nothing at all like him can ever have been heard on the air before, and never will be again. He really has tremendous personality on the radio, he creates a character which seems combined of ferocity and a sort of boisterous, ferocious good humour. I am told that he does not drink at all, but he has the mellow loose voice and the cheerful wandering manner of the habitual drinker. He talks on for hours always perfectly at ease, sometimes he stumbles over a word and corrects himself with a complete lack of embarrassment, speaks of 'these villainous *Fascistas*' and an agonised voice can be heard behind him correcting him, '*No, no, mi General, Marxistas.*' 'What difference does it make' – says the general and sweeps grandly on – ' – Yes, you *canalla* you anarchists of Malaga, you wait until I get there in ten days' time! You just wait! I'll be sitting in a café in the Calle Larios sipping my beer, and for every sip I take ten of you will fall. I shall shoot ten of you for every one of ours! (he bellows) If I have to drag them out of their graves to shoot them! – '

We were later told by one of the Italian journalists who had been present that he always broadcasted in full dress uniform with all his medals on, and that his staff similarly clothed were lined up behind him. It was from this group that there used to come those protesting voices when the general made some unfortunate slip. But it is impossible to give a good idea of Queipo de Llano on the air to those who have not heard him. He had a tremendous fascination for us, we could never resist him. He was like a tyrant in an old melodrama, he could 'tear a cat', as Shakespeare says. It was like listening to an old Drury Lane Tamburlane, it was like listening to Mr Punch. But unfortunately it was real.

I must not give the impression, however, that he was the only voice of Insurgent Spain, though he was our favourite performer, for we hardly thought of him as true; but Seville was much the most important Nationalist station then, Granada was inaudible, and most of the northern stations, shut away behind their high mountains, were nearly so. But I remember once hearing a speech from Seville by someone else, I have no idea who it was, which was very fine. The clear earnest voice with its beautiful Castilian accent was expressing noble ideas in noble words – through work, through sacrifice, we were to conquer, to increase men's welfare and happiness, to build a glorious new Spain. But Oh! how like the speech of the Anarchist I had just been listening to, it was: there were only a few words to be altered. For they were both the voice of the best thing in Spain, pure, passionate Idealism.

Chapter 5

WE WANTED VERY MUCH to go into Malaga to see with our own eyes what had happened there; but for the first day or two after the rising no one was allowed to enter the town limits without special permission and a very good reason for asking for it. Anyway the trains and buses were not running so that getting there and getting back again might have been difficult. Also we found that the servants became very upset when we spoke of going, so we put it off. But by the third day we began to get impatient and feel that we really must see something for ourselves, so we sent Enrique down to the village square to find out if there was any means of transportation. Even if there were not we thought one of the endless stream of lorries passing by might well give us a lift. However Enrique returned saying that the buses and trains were running again though not so frequently, so after lunch we started off. We found that buses were indeed running, but not the same buses; before the rising they had been fairly new and good, now the one that stood waiting appeared to have been rescued from some car dump. It was paintless, lightless and hornless, and when it started we discovered that it was also brakeless. However we were glad to find any bus at all, so we got in, and after much preliminary cranking and cursing, it finally moved off, trailing a cloud of thick black smoke behind it; but once started, rushed away at surprising speed. It pulled up with difficulty at the usual stopping place outside the big market, once the docks of the Moorish city, though now far from the sea, and still declaring in Arabic letters carved in the arabesque scrolls of its façade, '*Allah Alone Is Great*'.

We had stopped beside the stalls of the fruit vendors, and I was somehow surprised to find that they were as full and rich as ever. Fragrant Malaga muscatels, peaches and large purple plums seemed to be the most desirable fruits of the season, and I made a mental note to buy a big basket on my way back and fill it there. But though the fruit looked as luscious as ever we noticed that no one was coming to buy it; apart from the old women who kept the stalls there was hardly anyone about – I did not see a single woman in the streets near the market, the usual cheerful bargainers had disappeared. The streets were empty, and as we went along them we noticed that the cafés and shops we passed were all shut and barred. We turned off from the poor shopping streets and went through a little alley into the Alameda, a broad avenue with trees and flower-beds down the centre; it looked just the same except for the unusual emptiness, so we walked along it until we came to the end where there was a sort of square formed by its junction with the Calle Larios; on the corner of this stood the Casa Larios, the headquarters of Malaga's principal industries. It had been a big modern office building: it was now an ugly smoking shell. The streets had been cleared, but the roped-off sidewalks were still blocked with rubble and twisted iron from the window bars. From here we could see the beginning of the Calle Larios, Malaga's most important shopping street, and it was smoking and full of rubbish too. We began to walk warily like cats sensing danger.

We had stopped to examine the ruins of the Casa Larios, and found ourselves surrounded by the groups of people who were hanging about it. Furtively I examined them, and saw with a shock that they all looked quite mad. Just then an old workman came up to us, he was a rough powerful-looking old man, but had a twisted, crippled hand, in the other he was carrying a great bar of rusty iron. 'Look! Look!' he said grinning and brandishing the bar of iron in our faces, and pointing at the ruins with his crippled hand – he was drunk, and maudlin with pleasure in destruction.

I looked at the other faces around us and all looked queer and wild. The burning of the houses had been an orgy, and they were still completing their satiation among the ashes. Arson, I am sure, is a vice of the nature of an erotic crime: it is rape on the grand scale. The mad faces in the streets of Malaga seemed drugged with the lust of burning; and all the queer creatures of the gutter and the cellar, the twisted, the perverse, and the maimed had crawled up into the light of the flames.

We got away from the mad old workman and the dazed staring faces as quickly as we could and went on up the Calle Larios; there we found that only about half the houses had been burnt. Some were completely gutted, some only partly destroyed; there was a horrid smell of ashes and cinders and burnt iron like the smell of burnt-out grates. Rubble and bricks and twisted iron littered the pavements and in some places covered half the streets. Groups of calm, intelligent-looking young workmen were going about quietly repairing the damage as far as they were able, carrying away the rubble from the streets and sidewalks in carts, roping off the more dangerous places, taking down parts of the walls where they seemed to be too undermined to be safe to leave standing. A truck with a wrecking-crew from one of the garages was dragging away the wreckage of three or four motorcars.

It was reassuring to see these sensible young men going about their work in this quiet, efficient manner. For, apart from these busy workers there were very few people about except the crazy creatures who wandered from one ruined house to another. And I confess that I thought that the atmosphere was ominous in spite of the calm, helpful workmen. The city was evidently in a state of fear, and the people were staying close at home in their houses.

I only saw one person I knew there, a boy who worked for the grocer we dealt with. This grocer was an unpopular man, an Asturian of a rather disagreeable temper, very conservative in his sympathies and apt to hold forth on his opinions. We had already heard that his shop had been sacked during the house burning; nothing had been stolen; but sweets, hams, liqueurs, sugar, coffee, chocolate – all the luxuries most desirable to the half-fed men who were handling them – piled in the middle of the street and burned. The shop itself was not damaged except for the breaking of door and window because it belonged to some inoffensive citizen – 'And why should we ruin that poor man who never did us any harm?'

It was symptomatic of the time that the grocer's boy and I did not speak to each other as we would ordinarily have done. He looked at me without bowing but with recognition in his face, then he looked at the ruins and looking back at me slightly shook his head: I, too, looked at the ruins and back at him with an expression in which I tried to convey some of the regret I felt, and having exchanged all that we had to communicate we passed on still without speaking.

We wanted to get away from the Calle Larios with its ashes and ugliness, and go somewhere where we could get some news and also if possible some coffee, or even some water, for the heat and ashes made us terribly thirsty. All the cafés and restaurants were shut, so we decided to try the English Club. On the way there we met an Englishman we did not know, but remembered seeing around Malaga; we thought he was the owner or manager of some factory or business, I do not know what. Seeing English faces, he stopped to speak. He was haggard and dishevelled and seemed dreadfully upset.

'My God! This is terrible!' he began. 'They burned all the houses round us in the Caleta the other night. My children were in hysterics. Thank God, I'm getting them off on a destroyer. I don't know what my workmen will do – '

His agitation distressed us, and though we felt very sympathetic we wanted to escape from it. The poor man was obviously having a horrible time; I don't know why we should have wanted him to be dull and phlegmatic about it. He began to tell us a rather confused story about a Miss Someone-or-other who had just escaped with her life and lost all her clothes in the fire. The way that she had just escaped with her life seemed to be that she had been politely warned that they were going to set fire to the building where she was, and had walked out of it before the fire was started. It reminded me of some character in fiction who just escapes with his life by not being present at the battle of Malplaquet. But I suppose it seems worse for British subjects to lose their luggage than lesser races their lives.

We left the poor Englishman with our sincere wishes for the best, for we could not help thinking that a factory was going to be a doubtful and dangerous possession in Malaga for some time to come. The club was open and we had some very refreshing tea, but we were disappointed to find only one Englishman, an engineer whom we did not know, who had just come down from the sierra to get some money to pay his men and found all the banks closed and heavily guarded. He said that everything was perfectly quiet in the mountains so far, and knew even less about the rising than we did.

We were surprised to find that, though the club is on the third floor, all the windows had been shattered by bullets and a large engraving of Queen Victoria had got one in the eye. It seemed to explain the rather curious fact that only about a dozen people had been killed by all the hundreds of thousands of rounds of ammunition which had been fired on the first day.

'How many houses did they really burn?' we asked the steward, a nice man who was lucky enough to be a Rock Scorpion born in Gibraltar and consequently the fortunate possessor of a British passport.

'Half the Calle Larios, that's two or three blocks of houses, thirty or forty villas in the Caleta–Limonar district, and a few other houses in different parts of town.'

'What about Granada, is anything certain known?'

'Well, they say the Insurgents have succeeded, but that the Albaicin (the poor quarter) is still fighting. They say the Insurgents are entrenched in the Alhambra with two companies of Artillery and some guns – but it's all rumour. The Granada broadcasting station is silent, destroyed in the fighting, I suppose.' And Granada was never heard from. But I was told later that that was because it was a weak station and its waves could not pass the tremendous barriers of Sierra between us.

There did not seem anything more to be learnt at the club, and Malaga at the moment was certainly not a place to stay in for pleasure so we went off to get our bus. I tried as we went to buy coffee at various small shops on the way, but they were all shut with doors and windows locked and barred. 'They'll probably be open tomorrow,' a worried-looking Guardia Civil told us. Our bus was ready to start and already crowded to the brim when we got to the market, but the driver obligingly waited while I bought my basket and hurriedly filled it with fruit from the nearest stalls, then he somehow crowded us and the basket in; the country people with their usual good humour and good manners squeezing themselves into smaller and smaller space to make room for us.

'*Que lastima de Calle!*' everyone was saying: 'What a pity about the Calle Larios!' In our village at any rate the destruction in Malaga was not at all approved of, they thought it only showed how ill-behaved townspeople are.

When we got home we found the servants standing in the doorway looking out anxiously and much relieved to see us at last. They said it had seemed such a long time and they couldn't help thinking of awful things that might have happened to us. They did not trust the people of Malaga, wicked dwellers in large capitals that they were.

Poor Pilar was very much upset when I told her that our favourite shop for dress lengths had been burned.

'Oh! Señora,' she said. 'They might as well have given us some if they had only known. Why all the poor girls in Malaga might have had dresses with what they've destroyed like that!' I think she really felt more for the innocent pretty silks and cottons blackening and withering in the fire than for all the people who had lost their possessions or even their lives. In fact her feelings were those of an artist or at any rate of a connoisseur.

Chapter 6

W E WERE LATE IN GETTING UP on the morning after our trip into Malaga, even the rushing of the lorries failed to do more than slightly disturb our dreams; for we had returned very tired and then had been unable to tear ourselves away from the voices of the radio until a late hour. It seemed to me as I dressed that there were fewer lorries on the road, fewer sounds of enthusiasm. I met Enrique doing something to our innumerable pots of flowers as I passed through the patio on my way to the kitchen, and spoke of this impression I had had. He replied sardonically that it was because all the lorries were getting smashed up in accidents or ruined for lack of oil, water, and attention.

'Soon there'll be none left when they really begin to need them,' he said with the usual Spanish gift for disillusionment.

I went on out into the kitchen where Maria was trying to make the water for our coffee boil, fanning the charcoal with a palm-leaf fan; the charcoal as usual glowing sullenly and producing little heat. I waited idly talking to the company in the kitchen, which was crowded as it always was now with old women, young women, children and babies. They were all in terror of the Moors, and afraid to stay in their own houses. I tried to reassure them, telling them that everyone said that the Moors were still near Algeçiras and showed no signs of coming towards us at all; but they would not believe it.

'They will come and cut off everyone's heads,' they said. They asked me if they could come to us at the fatal hour, and I said, yes, of course they could come, we would fill the house with them, the garden, too, if necessary, fly the English flag, behave quietly, and nothing would happen to any of us. The Moors, I told them, were soldiers with officers, they were not going to attack an English house (I hoped this was true) – but anyway the Moors were not anywhere near us and were not coming any nearer. The thing to do was not to be frightened, but to go on with their own occupations as usual. I left them a little calmer, and as the coffee was ready at last went out to join Gerald in the garden for breakfast.

It was already set out on an old green café table, with a marble top, our invariable, always delicious, breakfast, of strong black coffee with hot goat's milk, marmalade made from our own bitter oranges and toast made from the marvellous Spanish country bread – bread so good that the Spaniards instead of saying *As good as gold*, say *As good as bread*.

We were sitting in our usual place beside a bed of brilliant zinnias: flaming dahlias and tall cockscombs flared in the sunlight around us, but we sat in the dense shade of two large Japanese medlars and looked out of their shadow at the autumn flowers glowing in the morning sun. The sound of the lorries hardly reached us there; it was the most peaceful moment we had had since the war began. But it was not destined to last for long, before we had even finished our coffee a messenger arrived with a letter from an English friend in Torre-molinos. In it she said that she had been asked by the Consul to get word to us that there was a destroyer leaving that afternoon, which was taking off English people and other foreigners to Gibraltar, that the Foreign Office wished to impress on English subjects the danger of their situation and the possibility that there would not be another opportunity of leaving, etc., etc. Our friend then resumed her own voice and invited us to come to lunch, a farewell lunch if we were staying as she was going, had been leaving soon anyway, or a fortifying lunch if we were all to join the crowd on a small destroyer.

We talked it over while the messenger was being refreshed in the kitchen. We had never really thought about leaving before. We had always felt (and we were right) that we were perfectly safe among these dangerous 'Reds' the Foreign Office was painting in such lurid colours, they were not going to do anything to us; we had never injured them, nor were we associated in their minds with any class of people or institutions which had. We did feel however, that our house and land was safer with us in residence. If there were a real revolution from the Left and it reached a point where confiscation began, a big empty farmhouse with fertile gardens and orchards and plenty of water for irrigation was an obvious thing to confiscate, or at any rate to put several peasant families in.

But we could not imagine their turning out two perfectly friendly English people. Then there were the house-burning tendencies of the time to be considered though they appeared to have ceased. If they should burn our neighbour, Don Cristober's house after all, our house would certainly be in danger. If we were there to direct operations we could almost certainly save it; if not, it might well go too.

So we decided not to think of leaving unless things became very much worse. Everyone thought then that Malaga would probably be taken before very long, but we did not see why we should not stay through the taking. We might be able to help a few of the poor people through the difficult moment. We might also (this appealed to me very much) establish a small hospital to take care of the wounded and sick if there was fighting near us. Our house, I could see, was made for a hospital on a small scale. Its long whitewashed rooms with their high ceilings and big windows and cool smooth-tiled floors could be kept immaculate with little work, and would make splendid wards. The large garden with its fountains and fresh running water would help restore the convalescents. There was a bathroom with a good modern water-heater for which we luckily happened to have in a large supply of anthracite. I got quite enthusiastic while I was thinking of the possibilities of the house – Don José, the saint-like village doctor, would help us, the Village Committee would get some beds and bedding for us somewhere, perhaps a destroyer would bring us medical supplies from Gibraltar – so my mind ran on.

But at other moments when I had no project for being useful in mind to amuse myself with, and remembered that we had definitely decided to stay in Spain, I confess that my heart sank. I was not really afraid of anything happening to ourselves. I did not even believe that there was any immediate danger to our Spanish friends. We did not then know the horrors which were going to take place in Spain, the cruel murders by the terrorists among the parties on the Left, the brutal massacres by the extremists on the other side. And yet I *felt* something. William James had a theory that the subconsciousness of all men might flow together at a level far below ordinary knowledge and thought, so that we are all aware in the depths of our minds of the same things though we do not ordinarily realise it. Freud in one or two passages shows that he has had the same idea, as when he suggests that the dreams of people living in the same house might affect each other. And I think that at that time in Spain, I, and a great many other people, somehow knew that something was coming in Spain far worse than anything which we yet expected with our conscious minds. I could feel something ominous in the air that sometimes frightened me.

This feeling of apprehension passed like an uneasy wave through my mind as we sat finishing our coffee that morning, and subsided again below the conscious level. Pilar came and cleared the table, and we wrote an answer to our friend accepting her invitation to lunch, but declining to leave on the destroyer. But we did ask her if she could take a suitcase full of papers (just in case), the deeds of the house and so forth, with a few of my favourite shawls and ornaments. We found the messenger cooled and refreshed waiting in the kitchen and discussing with the servants all the latest alarms and rumours, while the old women sitting around in their dingy black dresses croaked a melancholy chorus whose refrain was always '*Los Moros!*'

The young man had come on a bicycle, and it was the first bicycle we had seen flying the Red Flag, in this case a small dirty bit of red ribbon. Later on every cart and bicycle, every cottage, pigsty and hencoop had one. '*Hasta los burros tienen sus banderas rojas!*' Maria said sardonically ('Even the donkeys are flying their red flags!').

We felt very reluctant to set out on that long hot walk again. Memories of how heavily the radio had dragged upon us during the last mile made us consult Enrique about hiring a donkey to carry the suitcase. The only difficulty seemed to be that there was a general strike going on so that it was not permissible to hire anything. I cannot imagine what the general strike was against – Fascism perhaps – or why anyone thought a general strike was going to help in conducting a war. Perhaps it was just too exciting to work. Anyway no one could hire us a donkey: but of course, Enrique explained, we could *borrow* one and send a present later. He went off to get one from a neighbour, while Maria crossly and unwillingly made us up the usual *merienda*. We heard her talking to the old women about us as we went away to pack our things. They had exclaimed at our rashness in leaving 'our own village' in such times. Maria declared angrily 'The English are afraid of nothing and nobody!' It was by no means praise, but an accusation of presumption amounting to *hubris*.

By the time we were ready Enrique had returned with the donkey. It was grey, and grey donkeys in Spain, as far as my experience goes, are invariably called Platera – a happy portmanteau combination of two ideas: silvery, and plateracky, both highly applicable to a rawboned grizzled ass. (Brown donkeys are naturally always called Moreno, Brown One.) I addressed this Platera by his natural name, and he turned his mild face and lifted his large ears.

Enrique announced that he was going with us, to manage the *burro*, and also to see the English battleship. He strapped the suitcase firmly on Platera's back, and said that as it was so hot I had better ride for a while; I did not like to refuse though there is nothing that I like less than riding donkeys. The Spanish *burro*, perhaps I ought to explain, is often a large animal almost the size of a small mule, and this one thought nothing of my weight, but plodded along indifferently and methodically whether I was on or off its back at the usual donkey rate of two and a half miles an hour. Enrique knew *burros* too well to make any serious efforts to hurry it, he only gave it a light thwack across its hindquarters from time to time not to let it think that it was entirely left to its own devices, and occasionally shouted at it '*Ahre! Burro!*' or simply gave a harsh long-drawn-out protesting cry of '*Buuuuuuuuurrrrrro!*' The donkey did not appear to notice him at all, it did not even flick its ears, but I begged Enrique for my sake not to beat the patient creature. It was obviously just a waste of strength anyway, we would have to adapt ourselves to its crawling pace, and we did, and our trip to Torremolinos appeared interminable; it was after one o'clock when we finally found ourselves walking down its long white street towards the sea.

As the bright blue water came suddenly in sight between the dazzling houses we all gave exclamations. A large motionless destroyer seemed to be painted on this vivid backdrop. We were too late! Abandoning Antonio and Platera we took the suitcase and rushed on as fast as we could to the fashionable English *pension* where the English had been told to assemble. To our relief we found that the garden and veranda looking out over the sea were still crowded and swarming with English and American people standing about or sitting on piles of luggage; they seemed excited and the throaty high middle-class voices buzzed together like an angry hive. 'What's the matter?' we asked the first acquaintance we saw, a young English painter who had a little villa below. 'Well, the destroyer has come for us, but she can't land a boat to take us off because the proper authority hasn't come from Malaga. She radioed Malaga for it but it hasn't come yet, and Spain being in a state of war she can't land a boat without a special order from Malaga to the local authorities. Everyone is telephoning, and the poor Consul is being blamed for everything.' There was in fact a sort of British Chorus declaiming:

'Disgraceful!'

'British Subjects!'

'Telephone the Consul!'

'Communists!'

'What are they going to do?' we asked.

'Oh! I suppose they'll just wait for permission. The real trouble is that she came before she was expected. They told us three o'clock.' Just at that moment the stationary destroyer which had been picking up her rejected launch puffed out a cloud of black smoke and started off full speed ahead for Malaga. There was a chorus of disappointed 'Ohs!' from the crowd in which we joined. Faces fell; we were being deserted, abandoned. A charming young man, apparently out of a Wodehouse novel, sprang forward and threw up his arm. 'Stop!' he shouted after the rapidly disappearing ship. We all laughed but we all sympathised too with his impotent anger which wanted to catch that deserting destroyer by the rudder and tie her to the shore. Exasperatingly she steamed rapidly away and soon grew small in the distance.

'Telephone the Consul!' everyone cried at once. The advice was quite unnecessary as the poor Consul had never been able to put down the receiver for a minute since the destroyer had first appeared, busy as he was trying to evacuate British subjects from mines, waterworks, ruined castles, prehistoric cave villages and all the other odd places the English get themselves into in Spain, and at the same time to refuse heart-rendingly to help the stream of poor Spaniards on the Right who begged him to help them to escape or to save some much loved son or husband. We heard a loud woman's voice going on and on into the telephone. 'You must do something about it at once! Very badly mismanaged – ' She came out at last, a large formidable creature. 'They should have sent a battleship,' she said. She sat down in a vacant chair and began a conversation about Communists.

Two English friends had come to join us on our comfortable curb,
Jan W. and her young daughter Janetta. It was delightful to be with
English people who felt as we did, and shared our horror of what was
happening, and even without the Spanish friendships and love of
Spain, that made the situation so painful to us, still were thinking
more of the people who were really suffering than of their own
temporary inconvenience. For the attitude of our fellow Anglo-
Saxons was one of the things which depressed us most during the Civil
War, in Spain, and even more at Gibraltar.

While we sat talking to Jan and Janetta we looked around at the
refugees. They were not the anxious, flying, possessionless creatures
one usually associates with that word, but well-fed, well-dressed
members of the richer classes who had had good breakfasts and
baths that morning and would most probably have them tomorrow
morning too. The Civil War was just an annoyance to most of them,
it was interrupting their vacations just when the bathing was at its
best. I saw not a trace in them of any realisation that something
was happening of shocking importance to the Spanish people and
probably to the world. In most of them the war appeared to affect
nothing but their egotism; and many of them were full of a sort of
huffy pomposity as if the war had been got up on purpose as a
personal offence to them.

I say the war made no impression on them, and it did not appear to
at the time, but on some of them it certainly did make a profound and
surprising one; for a few of the refugees taken off by that destroyer
(not I think any of our Torremolinos ones but some from Malaga
hotels), who had seen absolutely nothing except the smoke of some
burning buildings and suffered not the slightest hardship except I
believe missing their lunch and tea on the destroyer which was very
crowded, arrived in Gibraltar with the most amazing atrocity stories.
One educated man of reputable position said that he had seen a nun
burned alive in broad daylight in one of the public squares of Malaga.

I suppose these preposterous stories show that the Civil War did make some impression on the British refugees, though hardly a desirable one. (As a matter of fact no nun in Malaga was ever injured in any way. And months after the rising the nuns who worked in the hospitals were being publicly thanked in the newspapers for their kindness to the wounded.)

Near us as we sat waiting that morning a sharp young woman was haranguing a group of acquaintances on the subject of the reign of terror we were supposed to be experiencing. It seemed that a gang of Anarchists, or as she of course called them 'Communists', had come out from Malaga to burn the images in the local church; they dragged them out and broke them up and set fire to them, she said.

'Was no one killed?' her hearers asked hopefully. No, apparently not only was no one killed, but there was not the slightest disorder.

'Didn't the villagers protest or try to save the images?' No, they just stood looking on indifferently for a while and then went home to supper, and only the children stayed on to dance around the bonfire. It was all rather casual apparently and no one seemed to take much interest in it; even the Anarchists went about it in a matter-of-fact way as if it were a sort of hygienic duty they had to perform.

Her story was interrupted by the appearance of two polite young workmen in clean blue overalls who had come to tell us that they had succeeded in arranging everything, they were members of the Village Committee. The refugees were to join the destroyer in Malaga, there would be buses to take them in that afternoon; as the destroyer could not leave that day (she had to wait for refugees from other villages who could not arrive in time), they were to spend the night at an hotel on the outskirts of Malaga – it was perfectly safe, the Consul would be there, and there would be a guard of carabineros. Everything was arranged, everything would be quite all right. No one much liked the idea of spending the night in Malaga which did look rather an ominous place with its cloud of smoke. But there was nothing else to be done.

The crowd began to disperse in search of lunch. Just then our friend Madame Vandervelde appeared and carried us off for ours.

The high dark room we sat in was cool and the long glasses we drank from were cooler still and infinitely refreshing. Madame Vandervelde drew me aside for a minute to discuss the best disposal of some of the things which had to be left behind by various people. She picked up a big earthenware bowl from the sideboard, a beautiful thick, heavy thing with a greeny grey glaze. 'Could I possibly take this with me, do you think?' she asked me. 'But what is it?' I asked in my turn. It was certainly not an example of the Spanish pottery we were so fond of, could it be Chinese?

'*You* know –' she answered. 'It's Omega pottery. Roger Fry made it for me.' I looked at her and picked up the bowl silently, for I had loved Roger Fry, too. And what a strange place, what a strange moment in which to see the handiwork still surviving the death of its maker, of that Apostle of beauty and the intelligence. I put it down sadly. Here in my hand, it seemed to me, was a piece of that very civilisation of the Western World we are always talking about saving; and the destroyer was certainly not going to bother about saving it, and if a bomb fell on it something would be left, but not very much.

Our lunch was sad, for it was in many ways a leave-taking, a leave-taking of Spain as it had been and would be no more. Before we had finished our coffee there was a knock at the door. The buses had come to pick up the refugees and their luggage, so we hurried off again to the *pension*. The two ancient buses which had come were already so full that it was almost impossible to cram more people inside; but they were got in somehow by the good-natured workmen's committee, and with two fine-looking carabineros in charge they rumbled off almost too suddenly for leave-takings. Goodbye! Goodbye! *Salud! Salud!* They were gone, and we were left standing in the street with a few other die-hards who also would not desert their homes or businesses. There were also a few poor Germans and refugees of other nationalities who could not leave because they had no passports and nowhere to go. The departure of the English in many cases was taking away their only means of livelihood. How were they to live now, poor Ishmaels of our days!

We said Goodbye and Good Luck to the other stayers, and started down the street to the sea to bathe. As we passed all the villagers greeted us with friendly smiles, they were so pleased at our staying. They had felt the English going off as they did very much. There were the English, members of a stronger nation and they had to be taken off in destroyers – *Vaya!* – as if they were not perfectly safe where they were! Finding that some of the English had not gone and evidently felt safe among Spaniards comforted their injured pride, and also reassured them for themselves, making them feel that the situation really couldn't be so bad after all if we stayed on of our own free will. So that we received almost a minor ovation as we went down the crowded street, everyone smiling at us and old women coming out to pat us on the arm and say 'These ones aren't leaving, they aren't afraid to stay with us.' We smiled back at them feeling a profound attraction towards them, towards the Spanish people – not the Left nor the Right, but the people of Spain.

The bathing that afternoon was perfect, infinitely cool and refreshing. We swam about in the lovely salt green waves for a long time. Afterwards drying our feet and putting on our gritty cotton sandals we sat looking out to sea. A little squatty Spanish cruiser was going off towards the south somewhere on her occasions. The smoke from the city still drifted far out to sea. For some reason there was no one about except a few children further along the beach, there was not even a fishing boat to be seen along the shore.

We got up to go home at last. There was no one left, we rather sadly realised, to offer us tea or cocktails as we climbed back up the long white street. As we stood looking after the little destroyer steaming heavily away under the smoky sky, there was certainly rather a feeling of being marooned in the air.

Chapter 7

THE NEXT FEW DAYS showed a great improvement in the situation; train and bus services were resumed everywhere, and in Malaga the shops were opened and the streets began to look more normal though there was still a notable absence of women in them and also of well-dressed men. The necktie, symbol for some reason of bourgeois degeneracy – had completely disappeared, on Spanish necks at any rate, though some among the foreigners continued to wear them and to dress as usual. It was pleasant to meet, among the blue overalls and collarless shirts which became the fashion, Sir Peter Chalmers Mitchell in the smartest of summer suits and the brightest of button-holes. And I remember thinking that the American Consul, a large figure in starched and glittering white, was enough to discourage any revolution. Mr Clissold, the British Vice-Consul, was another who dressed exactly as usual. He was an admirable man for a difficult situation, and all the English in Malaga as well as many others had reason to be extremely grateful to him.

For a time we went into Malaga almost every day hoping to pick up some scraps of news, but we never got very much. British destroyers and gunboats came and went from Gibraltar continually (the Foreign Office had been rather previous in warning us that that first destroyer was probably our last chance of leaving, for there was an opportunity of going every few days, either on an English gunboat or destroyer, or from time to time on an American destroyer, or a French or German boat of some sort). They took our letters for us, as of course there was no ordinary post out, and occasionally brought us a letter or two, but most of ours seemed to get lost on the way. Some arrived rather ironically, one came from a friend in Germany I had not heard from for years, another from a missionary acquaintance who kindly sent us some lime seeds from Portuguese East Africa, later on another strayed in from Bali marked 'via Siberia'. Why these exotic communications arrived safely when our plain English post did not I have never been able to imagine. We did both send and receive cables.

It was pleasant meeting the young sailors from the destroyers and gunboats (it always is pleasant meeting sailors), but they never seemed to know even as much as we did about the situation in Spain. The thing they did know more about was atrocities, and they often left us gasping at the stories they told us they had heard in Gibraltar. The best (on the authority of a high official in Gibraltar) was that naked nuns were being crushed by steamrollers in the streets of Malaga. This Marx Brothers–Heath Robinson atrocity still makes me laugh when I think of it, it was such a completely inane invention.

Some German writers have recently most disinterestedly praised the British propaganda during the last War, the stories of handless babies, crucified Canadians, corpse factories, and all the rest of the manufactured evidence with which we fed the avid public. They point out that it was highly successful in rousing public feeling, and is an excellent example for them to imitate in the next war. That the feelings which it aroused were feelings more suited to maniacs or the lowest type of savages than to civilised human beings is a point which, I am afraid, neither they nor we will consider if there is another occasion when the usefulness of arousing the basest of human passions arises. But it is really hardly necessary to have a special office and pay experts to invent your atrocities. In time of war people are so changed and their uglier instincts are so actively at work that unpaid amateurs will do it for you.

It has constantly been suggested in the Press that the savagery with which the war in Spain has been conducted is due to the violence of the Spanish character: I do not really subscribe to that point of view. Spaniards, I would agree, *are* a race of stronger feelings than (for instance) the British or the North Americans. They not only hate more bitterly, they love more warmly; and that leads at times to violent outbursts of popular feeling, sometimes magnificent as in the universal resistance to Napoleon's armies, sometimes deplorable as in the murder of hundreds of harmless French men and women at that time. And it ought always to be remembered that this has been a Civil War of the bitterest kind, with the opposing ideologies struggling, inextricably mixed together in every town and village.

A great many people still remember England as it was in the last War (which was *not* a civil war and *not* fought on English soil). I cannot myself, for I was not only very young then but lived in the tropics where distance and security kept heads clearer, so that even at the height of the struggle the German members of the local Yacht Club still came to the clubhouse and were kindly received. I think it shows how much international relations have deteriorated of late years that this statement which would have been received as a matter of course by Wellington (read, for instance Napier's description of Soult's wonderful kindness to his brother, Major Napier, when he fell into his hands with a bullet through his leg, and his efforts to get him exchanged as soon as his leg was entirely healed so that his military career would not be affected!) always arouses surprise and often disapproval now.

But even those of us who cannot remember what the country was like then have heard a great deal about it from those who can. Many people who were soldiers then have told me that they hated to come home, they were so horrified by the bloodthirsty, suspicious, crazy state their friends and neighbours were in. For the soldiers are apparently always much saner in a war than the civilians. Hundreds of unpleasant incidents of the period, attacks by mobs on poor German shopkeepers, with difficulty saved by the police from their would-be murderers, the persecution of sensitive people whose crime was not to approve of war for religious or social reasons, attempts by mobs to burn houses of people with German names (who had frequently never even been in Germany), show only too clearly the state of the public mind. But all we really have to do is to look at a newspaper of the period – read now in cold blood, it is a painful spectacle.

In view of these few facts, and a thousand others which could be brought forward about the condition of England during the last foreign war, it is horrible to contemplate what it would be like in a state of civil war. And that, after all is what we are observing in Spain – and the worst kind of civil war, with religious feeling, class feeling, political differences, sectional feeling, all engaged – any one of which in the past has proved enough to embitter whole nations.

In many ways the conduct of the Spanish people, far from being worse than might have been expected from a population with all restraint removed (for the Civil Guards and the Guardias de Asalto were almost all sent to the front as the only trained men available) was very much better. After all, cities which have had police strikes have always had trouble of some sort, generally looting. Boston does not sound a very violent place, yet when its police struck they had to call out the Militia. And everyone remembers the alarm the General Strike occasioned in England.

Our village, which was a large one by English standards – it contained over two thousand people – was perfectly quiet, safe, and orderly during the entire Civil War, except when invaded on several occasions by gangs from Malaga. And it must have been typical of hundreds of other villages in Spain. It was managed by a Syndicalist Committee, a committee chosen by a meeting of the entire village and serving without salary.

In our village they were all Anarcho-Syndicalists. That is, everyone belonged to a Syndicalist trade union because everyone belonged to a Syndicalist trade union. One villager who did not was always known as 'that Antonio of the UGT' because he was a worker in a sugar factory and belonged to the UGT, a Socialist trade union which many of the workers in the sugar factories belonged to. It was regarded as rather marking him out, like being an 'Elk' in a community of 'Buffaloes'. But that there was any ideological divergence between them I don't think ever entered anyone's head. In fact there really wasn't any. Most of them weren't politically minded at all. And those that were were all Anarchists in the simplest and vaguest meaning of that word. That is, they were federalists, and believed in as little central authority as possible (or none) and the village as the unit of political life; in the natural rights and the natural dignity of man, to be respected in the poorest and most miserable; in some sort of communal possession of the land (this is a very old idea in Spain, formerly true to some extent in fact, and often advocated in the writings of the Church Fathers up to the eighteenth century), and – most important of all – they believe that man is naturally good, but has somehow fallen from his early Eden through the corruptions of the world; but left to himself (they think) in primitive surroundings he can always create the Golden Age anew out of the natural simplicity and goodness of his own heart. This faith seems to me so touching in itself and to show so clearly the simplicity and goodness of natures that profess it that I cannot help always feeling a sort of love for the anarchists in Spain.

But this sort of natural anarchism in Spaniards is something so truly Spanish and so common in Spain even in days before Anarchism was ever heard of and even among Spaniards who would call themselves now Conservatives or Republicans or simply non-political that there must surely be something truly indigenous to Spain about it. So that it seems to be not so much an expression of some new ideology as of the simple and noble nature of the Spanish character.

The Anarchists are generally credited with most of the crimes committed on the Government side in Spain (or – much more horrible! – the crimes supposed to have been committed there, though in the foreign Press they are usually referred to as the 'communists'.) That there have been terrorists among the Anarchists is perfectly true. Unfortunately there have been terrorists among most of the political parties in Spain – what they call their 'uncontrollables'. But the Anarcho-Syndicalists as a whole while they are sometimes unable to control the excesses of the criminal elements which are apt to spring up among them in bad times (partly due to their not believing in restraining the natural impulses of man and not having any means of restraining them if they turn out to be bad after all) are, as one would expect, anti-militarists and against violence in general.

But unfortunately there is nothing new and nothing peculiar to one party about terrorism in Spain (I wish there were!). The Napoleonic Wars had their own tale of cruelty and horror in those days, excesses were committed by both sides in the Carlist Wars, and in our own days we have seen this bitterest of civil wars with murders and mass executions in almost every part of Spain.

As I say our village was controlled by the 'Committee', and it was very well managed, quite as well as it ever had been. In fact it justified the old Spanish saying: *If you removed the central government in Spain no one would notice the difference*, and also, perhaps, the Anarchists' belief that if Central Governments were removed, in Spain, at any rate, each community would manage its own affairs happily and successfully.

There was perfect order, and respect for private property. There were, for instance, three or four large houses in the village belonging to rich landowners who did not live there, but came occasionally for short visits. These houses, though they belonged to individuals who were popularly suspected of Fascist sympathies, stood vacant during the entire period up to the taking of Malaga, even at a time when refugees from the interior were sleeping under trees in the rain. There was a suggestion at one time that some of the poorest people might be put in them, especially when bombs began to come through the thin roofs of their huts; but it was decided by the authorities in Malaga (and the village committee conformed to their decision) that as the big houses were furnished it would not be right to occupy them – the furniture might get hurt! Houses of people who were known to have left the country, however, were looted and occupied even in our village. And of course in Malaga where there was always an acute refugee problem, houses were occupied whether furnished or unfurnished. But I was speaking of our village and other villages I knew of.

There was something very touching in those days about the attitude of the more intelligent villagers. They were appalled by the catastrophe which had come upon them. They were not revolutionary themselves, and they felt that they had been abandoned and betrayed. And now power had been thrust into their hands, unwilling and unfit as they felt themselves to receive it. And they were pathetically anxious to learn how to use this new power as well as possible if they were called upon to do so, conscious as they were of their ignorance and lamenting their uneducated state. We had a great many friends among the masons and painters and carpenters of the village because we had had to have a good deal of *obra* (building and repairs) when we first moved into our house, and had been much impressed by the good work of the workmen we employed and by their good manners and frank and friendly ways, and as usually happens in Spain they had remained our friends after our need for their services was over. Some of them used to come in those days to try to learn something from us about this new problem of governing themselves. They asked us endless questions about England – was it true that even workmen sometimes owned *motorcycles* and that almost anyone could have a bicycle (a proud possession and an extremely rare one in our village) – did the villages govern themselves? Was it true that when men could not get work the Government helped them, and no one was actually starving? But then you are English, they would say, and know how to govern yourselves, and England is a rich country not like these 'poor worlds of Spain'.

I remember one day we stopped to talk to some masons who were mending a wall. 'But, Don Geraldo, have you seen what they are doing to us' (several people had been killed that morning in the neighbourhood by bombs) 'and we never did anything to them!' Later on I heard this used as an excuse for the gang murders in Malaga and the shooting of prisoners after air raids, but always half-shame-facedly – 'They are worse, they do worse things to us –' 'And they are *educated* men,' they would add sadly. 'What can you expect of us, poor ignorant creatures that we are! But they had opportunities and went to schools and universities – and see how they are behaving, worse than we do!'

Often, if we happened to go out during the evening and found the usual gathering in the kitchen, some poor visitor would say: 'Why doesn't England put her hand to Spain? We will never do anything for ourselves. The English are good, but we are bad, bad, *somos malos, malos!*'

For the Spanish poor, at any rate, we occupy the place the Germans did for the Romans in Tacitus's pages. Stupid and noble, calm, heavy-drinking, nature's noblemen – we are the stick they use to beat each other with.

'See the Germans how much nobler they are!' Tacitus was always saying. 'Honest, chaste, handsome, brave (though stupid, drunken gamblers all, I grant you!). Why aren't you more like them, ignoble, modern Romans!'

I daresay the Romans left behind them in Spain their old custom of telling each other how much better the blond northern races are – (only it's a pity they are *quite* so stupid, they add under their breath). We had got used to feeling large and stupid and honest – the size and stupidity we always found quite easy and even the honesty was not very difficult in a country where our only business transactions were buying grapes for a penny or lettuces for a farthing, and having Maria assume the responsibility even for that.

Chapter 8

THE IMPROVEMENT in the state of things seemed to be continuing, and we began to hope that some arrangement would be come to between the various parties. We even hoped that perhaps the military *coup* had not really come off after all, and also that the Government would be able to dominate the revolutionary forces which seemed to be coming to the front. After all there had been so many military *coups* in Spain and so many revolutions, and so few of them had come to anything. Our village continued perfectly quiet, and in Malaga everything appeared almost normal on the surface, but we began to hear sinister rumours of continual arrests and nightly murders by gangs in the city and also in some of the villages near us.

The Province of Malaga had practically become an independent state with almost the old limits of the Moorish Kingdom of Malaga. The little trains ran but they did not run very far, the posts arrived and went out, but they only went to a few places. Granada, Algeçiras, Cadiz, Seville had all become enemies and everyone thought in provinces – a Spanish habit at the best of times.

'Granada is attacking us,' people said. 'Seville is attacking us.' The capture of a town in the province of Granada was regarded as putting us one up on Granada. We had scored; and it was seriously suggested that the captured town should be incorporated in the Province of Malaga! This extreme federalism was more important to most of the country people than the class-war aspects of the struggle which some of their leaders were emphasising. They had always thought of the Granadinos as foreigners anyway, and there was nothing very surprising about their turning into active enemies.

Some of the villagers of course were very class-war conscious, and there was one remark which was common at the time which used to annoy me more than I can say. To my irritated ears it used to seem to go on all the time like a sort of chorus, and it was always spoken with maddening self-complacency. It was: 'You can do nothing against the will of the people!' And I used to think that anyone silly enough to make such a remark at such a moment ought not to be allowed any exercise of the will at all. Another remark which was also common and annoyed me only slightly less, and was made with almost equal self-complacency was 'If all the Provinces did their part as *we* have done it would be all over now. But now they want *us* to help them with their work.' I used almost to join Maria in her snort of contempt when some villager who had taken no part in the struggle and had no intention of taking part in it unless it actually broke out in the street he lived in and forced itself in at his front door, used unctuously to produce this piece of wisdom again.

Still I can't help thinking that it was really to the credit of the Malagueñans that they did not on the whole show any disposition for war. They were people of peace, and wanted to take as little part in this unnecessary struggle as possible. They never made any real attempt even to defend their city, which seems curious in Spain, the country of remarkable sieges. Malaga did not seem to us even at that time likely to be the scene of a second Numantia or Saragossa; and time was to prove that we were right.

But those appalling sieges for which Spain is famous, sieges which seemed designed to show how much human beings can force them-selves to endure without even hope to aid them, have always taken place in the *north* of Spain. Numantia, Saragossa, Gerona, the Alcazar at Toledo and of course Madrid, in the present war, and a dozen other sieges which could be named all occurred in the north.

I don't mean to suggest that Andalucians can't be extremely brave: they have proved their bravery in every war they have taken part in. But that extraordinary tenacity of whole populations, that screwing your courage to the sticking point and never wavering again, those forlorn hopes which last not for an hour, but for months of taut agonising endurance, that gaunt stoical holding-out against all rhyme and reason, that sublime, or demoniac, stubborn, desperate insanity of courage seems only to exist in northern Spain out of all the countries in the world.

'The Insurgents can take Malaga any afternoon they feel like it,' I remember Gerald saying at about that time. 'But I don't believe they will take it now, because from a military point of view they ought to get on with their drive north. Malaga isn't of sufficient strategical importance for them to spare the men to take it.' Of course we didn't realise then how many Moors would be brought, much less that there would be foreign intervention on a great scale.

Poor Gerald had had only too much experience of wars, for he had gone to Belgium as a boy of nineteen in the spring of 1915, and not returned to England except for short periods of leave and longer periods spent in hospitals until the summer of 1918 when he finally ceased to be passed for active service at the age of twenty-three. As one of his reasons for living in Spain (besides trying to recover his health) had been that it had been neutral in the last war, and so was not connected in his mind with a period he so much disliked remembering, it seemed curiously hard luck that we should have chosen a house on the edge of an unsuspected volcano.

One hot day when things seemed particularly quiet we heard the really alarming news that several thousand Moors had been brought over.

'I'd bring over an army in canoes!' snorted an English naval officer we happened to meet at the club, in disgust at the inefficiency of the officerless Spanish Government Navy, which seemed usually to be tied up to the dock in Malaga at that time.

The poor old women who hung about the kitchen were dreadfully upset at the news about the Moors, and their chorus of '*Los Moros! Los Moros!*' murmured on all day.

'Won't England help us against the Moors?' they used to ask pathetically. I don't think that they ever had the least idea of who was fighting or why. They had heard of old wars against the Moors, and thought that those evil days had returned. They had in any case no conception of what the world consisted of. They lived in a medieval world – there was Spain, or rather Malaga, and there was the sea, and they had heard that there were lands beyond the sea; but what lands, or what they were like they did not know. When we told them that England was cold and wet, they replied quite simply and understandingly 'Ah! you live in high mountains, but there is no doubt plenty of wood to burn there.' To explain why England was really cold and wet you would have had to begin at the beginning and reform the school system of Spain sixty years ago.

And so we could not easily explain why England would not help them now 'against the Moors' – we were rich, we had plenty of battleships, they had often seen vast grey boats flying the British flag coming up from the Straits – it would cost us so little – they sighed – and we sighed too over the impossibility of explaining to these poor creatures suddenly waking up in the midst of a civil war, why it was that Spaniards were killing one another.

But there were terrors even greater than the Moors coming for them. One morning we were quietly sleeping under a grey sky, for it was early morning and the blackness of the night was fading, when – CRASH! a large bomb had fallen out of the grey air, and after it came the sharp rattle of a machine-gun. We leaped from our beds before we even realised what the dreadful noise was. The loud drone of the plane overhead warned us that there was still danger about, and we rushed out, calling the servants as we went, and met Pilar carrying the sleeping Mariquilla and hurrying down the passage towards our room crying, 'Don Geraldo! Don Geraldo! What has happened?' There was a second terrific crash as we met, and we hurried her downstairs where we found Maria and Enrique who had run in half-dressed from their cottage, and led them all into the big storeroom where we hung the fruit. Its thick walls and the fact that it had only one small high window and that its only door opened into a long passage made it *seem* the safest place anyway.

There were two more terrific crashes, but the next sounded much further away. Maria muttered to herself, I don't know whether prayers or curses, Pilar quietly wept, rocking the sleepy, whimpering Mariquilla in her arms, Enrique as befits a man wrapped his coat stoically about his shoulders. Another crash was obviously at a considerable distance, and Gerald and I rushed up to the balcony to see what was happening.

A big silver-grey plane was hovering at a great height probably trying to hit the planes at the airfield. Artillery and machine-guns had begun to crash and rattle in Malaga. The louder crash of the bursting bombs came at intervals. They left tiny white puffs of smoke in the air as they fell (or were those from shells?). A fire blazed up suddenly near the sea – at the airport? But the planes had dropped all their bombs. Like silver flies they sailed away out to sea, towards Africa. Two little aeroplanes had got up from the field to pursue them, barking and coughing, obviously completely outclassed, but gamely willing to attack these deadly grey strangers. But the grey bombers out-flew them, grew tiny in the distance and disappeared, and the little coughing planes returned. Distant as we were they looked like noisy toys as they sailed in circles and finally settled down.

The next morning promptly at four, bombs again! as punctual and arousing as an alarm clock, and after that we were bombed almost daily for some time, generally in the early morning but sometimes later and occasionally in the afternoon; the night raids came later. After the first raid we all knew what to do, and were downstairs and gathered together in two minutes, but I refused to stay in the store-room, it seemed to me to resemble a tomb too closely; I preferred the corner of the dining-room though it was obviously not so safe a place, as it had a large window on the patio, but I think we all had an irrational feeling that the bombs would come to the front door instead of the back. Anyway the servants either through that belief or through blind confidence in us joined us in the dining-room and left the safer *despensa* to the more timid of the villagers who came seeking refuge.

For after that first air raid the lower floor of the house was always crowded with refugees. Our big house seemed so much safer to them than their own poor little cottages that all our poor neighbours rushed in with their children at the first rumour that planes were coming, or at the sound of some shots in the distance, and many of them spent almost the entire day in our garden too frightened to go home except to get a little food ready. We had one very large room opening off the patio which we gave up to them completely, and a number of them brought their bedding and slept in it after the night raids began. But as the air raids continued a great many villagers became too frightened to stay in the village during the day, and every morning there was a pathetic stream of frightened people carrying their children and driving their goats, going off to the mountains. I can still see in my mind the touching little Swiss Family Robinson groups and hear their shrill frightened chatter, as they hurried by looking up at the sky as they went fearful of seeing planes approaching.

I found later that Pilar and I had received the same impression from the little groups going to the mountains: we wanted to go too. Not then, but if things got very much worse and if 'the Moors were coming'. We found each other out in this, and used to enjoy planning it all. We decided that we would try to buy a donkey to carry our food and blankets, and a couple of milk goats to take with us, we would grind the maize which we had just harvested to make corn meal mush of, and buy as much flour as we could, and we would take the chickens, but would have to eat them soon as we could not feed them. The chief problem was 'Piggy', Enrique's pig, who like all Spanish swine was practically a household pet – should we take him on the hoof or in the form of hams and sausages? He was still small, but could we find enough acorns to feed him during our Robinson Crusoe life among the cork oaks. I regretfully decided that Piggy probably ought to be turned into sausages.

For I was much attracted by the vision of our expedition to the woods and the wilds accompanied by Platera, two brown nanny goats and Piggy; led by tall, fair Don Geraldo springing actively up the mountain with the goats and followed by severe black-clothed Maria acting as rearguard and turning back to lay a final curse upon the wicked city. Pilar and I could not help feeling that even after Piggy was disposed of, Maria might turn out to be an insoluble difficulty; so we rather tended to leave her out of our dream of desert island life in the sierra.

But often later on when things began to get worse, I used to wander off in my mind to the mountains – I would be sitting by a stream under an ilex tree with Piggy eating up the acorns on the ground, and the donkey and the goats cropping the grey, sweet mountain herbs, while Don Geraldo leaped from rock to rock above us looking for dangers and Enrique gathered sticks for the little fire on which the corn meal was cooking in a black iron pot, and Pilar sang Mariquilla to sleep with a Christmas *copla*.

> 'The Virgin hung her washing
> On the rosemary to dry,
> All the birds were singing
> And the river running by.'

Or I would imagine that we were just setting out, going further and further away from towns and men, weary and hungry, but climbing higher and higher into the clear, free, mountain air.

Air raids soon became almost a part of normal life. It is strange how quickly you become accustomed to them; and in a curious way when there was no air raid as sometimes happened I *missed* it. I was keyed up to expect it, and if it did not come I felt a sort of flatness. But our raids were not really bad ones, the bombs were usually small and we always felt that unless there was a direct hit on the house just above us, or unless we were hurt by flying splinters or glass we were fairly safe indoors; and Gerald and I were fortunate in both being of rather philosophic temperament and inclined to feel the bombs probably were not going to hit us and if they were we could not help it – and of course Gerald had had so many worse times in the last war already.

When huge modern bombs are being used I know from experience in Malaga when they were trying to wreck the port with them, it is impossible to be philosophic. The noise and shock are appalling and the feeling that there is no defence anywhere, that whole houses will fall upon you, is horrible.

What I really minded most about the air raids in our village was the terror of the villagers. Our servants were very stoical, but some of the women lost all control of themselves and sobbed and screamed hysterically, while the poor children, terrified by the behaviour of their parents as much as by the unknown horror of the sky, shrieked and sobbed convulsively. Something I felt then (and am ashamed to have felt) was a physical repugnance towards these poor frightened creatures, towards their lack of control which is always an ugly thing to see and to the sharp fetid smell which fear produces. I felt all the time that my sensations were meanly fastidious just when I should have felt the strongest solidarity with my fellow men. But I could not help that instinctive distaste and withdrawal into myself when outwardly I was being kindest and most reassuring. But there were times when the pain of these others melted the thin icicle in my heart (we need no Snow Queen, any of us, to put one there).

One day one of the village women was caught out of the village by an air raid while she was taking some food to her husband at the airfield. Her fear for herself alone in the fields with huge planes hovering overhead scattering death must have been very great, it must have seemed like a horrible nightmare to her, but her fear for her children was much greater, and she did not try to take cover, but ran all the way home to them. They had already come in to us and were crying 'Oh! Mother! Mother!' sure that she had been killed by the first explosions. When she rushed in, not having found them at home and desperate with anxiety and saw them sitting with me, she tried to take a few steps further to reach them and fell in a fit at my feet. As I knelt on the floor beside her while she foamed at the mouth and jerked and twisted in convulsions I felt not the slightest trace of repulsion. She was among the poorest of the women: she was dirty, emaciated, ugly, unkempt, ill-smelling – everything that man's inhumanity daily makes of man, except unloving or unloved. But as I sat there holding the poor creature in my arms as she gradually grew quieter and the fearful upturned eyes closed in unconsciousness, while her daughter sat beside me embracing her mother and sometimes kissing my helping hands, my mind held no tinge or taint of distaste, I felt nothing but love – for them and for the millions like them, the poor, the suffering, the burden bearers of this world.

One morning not long after the raids began we were waked as usual by the crash of a bomb: it was just beginning to be light. The bombs seemed fairly distant, so we went up on the balcony to see what was happening. The planes were dropping incendiary bombs, trying to hit the petrol tanks and the standing planes at the airfield: they caught the dry grass where they fell and blazed with much white smoke. Presently black smoke poured up from the airfield, probably one of the standing planes had been hit. Gerald brought out his field-glasses.

'I hope Don Carlos is all right,' he said, and then a moment later 'My God! They've hit his house!' Don Carlos was a poor but aristocratic Spanish friend who lived on some land he farmed near the sea, which actually adjoined the airfield. Now his house was hidden by clouds of white smoke.

'Oh! the children!' I said. I imagined them burnt by the bombs, trapped in their rooms.

'We'd better go at once,' Gerald said. I seized a basket and put in bandages, iodine, and a bottle of brandy and Enrique said that he would come with us as we might need him, and we set off.

I have to confess (and I am again ashamed to confess it) that I enjoyed that walk. There was just enough feeling of danger in the air to give me a feeling of heightened life, of using some faculty that generally sleeps. Dawn was coming over the sea and we were walking towards the growing light. And we walked rapidly, seeming almost to fly as one sometimes walks in dreams.

A patrol hailed us and we stopped to explain where we were going.

'Two boys were killed at the San Fernando farm,' they told us. 'A bomb fell right on them as they were standing in the patio drinking some milk the farmer's wife had given them, the bomb fell and – *nada* – ' They made a gesture of dispersal – *nothing*. They just happened to be there. It was chance – *and what of those six on whom the Tower of Siloam fell* – my mind asked retreating from the thought of those too near, too recently shattered, bodies. Well it will be *our mala sombra*, our ill-shade, if one of these bombs catches us and poor Enrique while we are rushing away across these early morning fields. And yet I could not repress that lift of excitement, of happiness, as if quicker, more ardent life were running through my veins, or as if I had been drinking some wine not meant for me but for creatures of more fiery birth.

I hate war, I have a perfect horror of it; and what little of it I saw in Spain confirmed me in my fear and hatred. And yet after that early morning walk across the fields I understood, better than Bertrand Russell could ever explain it, *Why Men Fight*.

And when we got near Don Carlos's house we saw that it was not on fire at all! Two incendiary bombs had fallen near it, one on an empty chicken house in the backyard and the other in some dry grass and both were still burning and sending off great clouds of white smoke. But the house itself was untouched and we could see figures moving calmly about. We went on anyway; we had other reasons besides the danger of bombs to make us anxious about Don Carlos and his family.

We crossed the main Algeçiras road and reached their gateway and Don Carlos and his family came to meet us full of surprise at seeing us there at five o'clock in the morning, and full of gratitude when they found out that we had come to rescue them, however unnecessarily. They were excited but not at all frightened. Don Carlos was tall and florid and slightly bald, and always somehow reminded me of a charming, aristocratic, Spanish Wilkins Micawber (if such a combination can be imagined!); he had spent a lifetime of difficulties but was always full of hope that something was 'just going to turn up'. He had been in Chile and Tierra del Fuego for years, where he was sheep farming, acting as consul for other South American countries, and in fact doing anything that 'turned up'. Don Carlos and his family particularly attracted me because they reminded me of my half-brother and his family who lived on the cotton plantation he had inherited from our father (where I was brought up) in a state of extraordinary happiness and improvidence, with half a dozen riding horses and no money to speak of.

Doña Maria Louisa, I might as well say without mincing words, was almost the nicest woman I ever knew anywhere. Tall, fair and handsome, a devoted wife, mother, daughter, friend, very kind, and courteous and friendly with rich man, poor man, beggar or thief. The whole family were gay and amusing, and Don Carlos had the Spanish genius for telling a story and for making gossip and personalities interesting and vivid, and somehow universal in their application. Their children were charming too; there were two nearly grown-up boys and two nearly grown-up girls and little Emilio who was only six.

'Have you been all right here?' we asked Don Carlos rather anxiously. He was unfortunate in having a famous name, though he had not inherited much besides, except this strip of land along the sea on which he had built a small house and a part share in the family house which we had bought from him and other members of the family. But a famous name at that period brought death to a great many harmless and innocent people. One of Don Carlos's nephews, a boy of eighteen, was taken away and shot because he had this too well-known name and because only a few weeks before he had got a small place as clerk in Malaga's principal industry which was managed and partly owned by a distant cousin. The cousin was shot as a matter of course after spending a few weeks in prison. He deserves to be remembered for he was a brave man. He was safe in hiding but gave himself up when some of the men under him were put in prison, and tried to take upon himself the entire responsibility for the conduct of the firm, which had been having trouble with strikers. But I'm afraid they were all shot anyway. I liked his last words, they were: 'Do you mind if I light a cigarette?' He lit it and took a few puffs and then gave the signal to fire, himself. Having a feeling even then that famous names were going to be a fatal possession in Malaga we were worried about the C— family (on both sides they had a great deal of English blood and used English names) even apart from their living so unfortunately close to the airfield.

'Come and stay with us,' we urged them.

'Seven of us!' said Maria Louisa, 'and we can't leave the chickens – but how good you are!'

'Do you really think you're safe?' we asked bluntly. 'What about your name?'

'Oh! but I've never done anything; I've been in South America half my life, and I've never taken any part in politics. Why should they do anything to me?' said Don Carlos. 'I'm a poor man too; the boys work as hard as peons, and we always get on well with the country people.' We knew that that was true, but we were not thinking of the country people but of the gangs in Malaga.

'Well, come any time,' we said. 'We'll always be expecting you. And bring as much as you can in the car. Why not bring the best chickens (they had prize Rhode Island Reds). You could bring a lot of them, you know we've got that huge fowl-house with only a few old hens in it. Do come! Fill up the car and come on over this very morning.'

'The car!' Don Carlos began to laugh. 'Did you see the burnt remains of something along the road: that was the poor old Buick! The Anarchists came to get it. Well, you know what the poor old car was – Pepe and Carlete and I could just start it all working together. You had to know its ways. Of course the Anarchists couldn't start it at all. They cranked it and cranked it and pushed it down the road, and finally they got so angry they put a match to the petrol and Poof! there it is! Poor old thing, it was a pity.

'But they gave poor Maria Louisa and the children a dreadful fright when they came for it – two lorries full of pistoleros bristling with rifles and revolvers. All of them got out and came up to the door, poor Maria Louisa was sure that they had come for me. I was in Malaga. But no, everything was politeness, they only wanted the car, they were requisitioning all private cars. The children warned them what a dreadful old crock it was, but they would drag it off.'

As we stood in the garden saying goodbye, a constant stream of lorries and commandeered cars kept passing by. The house was only fifty yards from the main road: we did not like it at all.

'Do come to us,' we urged again as we went away. Doña Maria

Louisa stood smiling and waving goodbye with the girls and little Emilio while Don Carlos and the boys walked to the road with us. What admirable things courage and self-control are, I thought, especially when combined with cheerfulness and good manners. For that smiling family we left behind must have realised even more clearly than we did, and felt – how much more poignantly – the loneliness and danger of their situation in that isolated house, too far for any help to reach them even if there were any help for them in those days, with the armed lorries rushing by and bombs falling out of the air above them.

Chapter 9

I THINK IT WAS ON THE DAY when we tried to rescue the C—s that I first noticed a new presence in the garden. I had been vaguely aware once or twice before of a tall young man rather good-looking in a mild ineffective way, who seemed to be always sitting about in the kitchen with an aged rifle which was generally stood in the corner like an old umbrella. And one day I asked Pilar who he was.

'Oh! he is one of the village guards on this part of the road. He is a foreigner, he comes from Guachas, that poor mountain village. He came down trying to get work but of course there isn't any work, so they've given him an old rifle and put him to guard our street.'

'Is he any use as a guard?' I asked sceptically.

'*Claro que no!*' replied Pilar smiling. 'He's a good young man. He knows nothing about shooting people; it's as much as he's ever done if he's shot a rabbit in the sierra.'

'Does he get paid for guarding us?'

'No, I don't think he gets anything.'

'Well, give him a meal sometimes,' I said. Here Maria gave a disapproving snort. Good Spanish servants defend their master's property almost to the death from shopkeepers who charge too much or weigh out too little, hucksters who charge a farthing a pound more than the lowest price possible to buy at, beggars who want food or money, and even, we think, guests, when possible to do so without injuring the honour of the house. Maria, I know, disapproved of our having so many visitors to stay and threw up her eyes to heaven when she talked of our housekeeping expenses. So I thought it quite natural and even proper that she should snort at the very idea of giving food to a strange young man from Guachas.

Later that evening I was walking in the garden. Standing on the little *mirador*, a small landing cut in the thick garden wall, with steps up to it, from which to admire the view, I saw Pilar silhouetted against the evening light. But who was that with her? I strained my eyes and saw, more by the light of sudden comprehension than by the fading twilight that it was the young man from Guachas.

Maria had plenty of excuse for snorting in the days that followed for the young man, whose name like that of almost every other male Malagueñan, was Antonio, proved to be a fixture. At all hours he was to be found either in the kitchen with the old gun standing against the wall while he sat watching Pilar cooking and washing up, or walking about with her in the more distant parts of the garden. I tried to talk to him and make friends with him, and he was friendly enough, but he seemed dull, *soso* as the Spaniards say, saltless, flat. It didn't seem to me that Pilar was really much taken with him either; she said frankly that he was dull and had nothing to say, but that he was 'very good'. But she was so pleased, poor Pilar, at having an admirer. She looked younger, happier, fresher; she wore her nicest clothes every day, my old cast-offs, carefully washed and mended, and combed and sleeked her straight black hair more and more smoothly and stuck flowers over her ear like a young girl. My poor Pilar, it was your 'one fair day'. There was something so touching about this late, thin blooming, and about all their timid, humble courtship – for they both belonged to the 'despised and rejected of men', 'the insulted and injured', and they were both like all the Spanish poor more acquainted with grief and hunger than with pleasure or plenty.

'Perhaps you'll marry Antonio,' I said one day.

'No,' said Pilar. 'We would have children and nothing to feed them. To be a poor mother is a misery. To listen and hear your children crying for bread. I have one child to keep already, and I will not take her to the house of hunger. She shall be brought up in your shadow, and never know the hunger and want I have known.'

But even this quiet gentle courtship which seemed unlikely ever to turn into anything stronger was made a source of torment to Pilar by her mother. Maria disapproved intensely. I do not think she said anything to the young man: he was a guest of the house, I suppose. But she scolded Pilar continually. There were several reasons for her disapproval. The young man was extremely poor and came of a very poor family, and for Pilar to marry him would be a going back from the life of plenty and respectability they had won at last, to poverty and uncertainty again. Then Maria was jealous – jealous, I think, in several ways, but chiefly of her ascendancy over Pilar and possession of her and the little girl which was threatened – why Pilar might even take Mariquilla off to Guachas and starve her there for all she could tell. Then there was a most curious objection peculiar to the Spaniards of the Alpujarras and of other very remote and out of the way districts, and that is that they disapprove of a widow or widower ever marrying again. There is, as far as I can make out, a feeling that it is improper and also a feeling that it offends the Universe and brings misfortune to the community. But it is only legal marriage which has this unlucky effect: a widow or widower can live with any one they like and no one pays any attention.

Anyway there was more than a trace in Maria of this odd prejudice. But I think that if the marriage had been an advantageous one Maria would have got over all her objections. After all grandchildren to an elderly Spaniard are the most desirable thing in life.

It was the second day after we had been to rescue the C—s: the evening had closed in and we were sitting in the big *sala* waiting for the lights to come on so that we could try to get some news on the radio, when we heard strange voices and a stir outside. Maria appeared in the doorway looking mysterious.

'They have come!' she declaimed in low intense tones like an old-fashioned Lady Macbeth.

'Who have come?' we asked startled. Could it be the Moors after all?

'Don Carlos and all of them, even the dog.' We hurried out and found all of them, 'even the dog' as Maria had said, a charming black-faced mastiff called Bull.

'We were afraid to stay tonight,' Maria Louisa said as we embraced. 'They say there will be a bad raid tomorrow, and there were so many bombs near us today. And there are so many armed lorries on the road and they keep stopping. I wouldn't mind for myself – but it's the girls. Could we just spend tonight with you?'

'Tonight and every other night,' we said. They had come secretly across the fields in the dusk, and they had the anxious excited look of people escaping from danger. We were glad to get them under our roof; for their situation had been very much on our minds ever since the rising.

They had brought two of their big red chickens for our supper, and the two girls and the younger boy sat down to pluck them while Maria prepared the rest of the meal, and Pilar and I searched the house for enough linen to go round and tried to make the beds stretch to hold seven additional people; with one borrowed one and a pallet on the floor for Emilio we finally managed it.

I went out to the kitchen once or twice in spare moments, and found the C— children talking to Maria and the usual crowd of kitchen guests as if they were all old friends. The Spaniards really believe and really practise their belief that our common humanity is enough to make friends and associates (or enemies and associates as sometimes happens) of us all. They can always talk to one another about something, even if they have never met before and come from different social worlds. Our all being human beings, they feel, gives us plenty of subjects for conversation. And the poor but aristocratic C—s and the poor labourers in the kitchen chattered

The household at Churriana in 1936: Rosario, Antonio, Miranda , Isobel (sitting) and Maria

away to each other with the greatest interest and animation. Fortunately the villagers did not seem to regard the children, at any rate, as *Fascistas* but as fellow sufferers under a rain of bombs.

In a surprisingly short time supper was ready: a grand chicken supper of a nature quite unusual in our quiet kitchen where our standard of life was kept low by Maria, who rather disapproved of people eating at all, and thought eating chicken was certainly a venial sin, if nothing worse. It was an exquisite night, and we sat in the patio after supper listening to the cool falling of the fountain and smelling the lovely fragrance which seemed to be opening and spreading like a gigantic flower in the dark. We could distinguish the scents of the jasmine on the wall, and of the magnolia-like datura, and the incredible sweetness of the dama-de-noche.

The relief of being safe in the peace of the old garden where the house shut out almost all the sounds of the rushing traffic in the street, made the C—s very gay, and we spent a delightful evening. They went at last to their rather inadequate beds; and we wandered round the garden as we almost always did before we could tear ourselves away, going from flower to flower like two perfume-drugged moths.

The next morning after breakfast our guests began making polite attempts to leave. No, they could not think of staying, so many of them – it was an imposition – indeed they could not! And there were the chickens which must be looked after. But we would not hear of their leaving, we were only too glad to have them safe under our roof. There had been no raid that morning, but there was sure to be another soon. And all our instincts (and in time of danger the instincts begin to work in quite a new way) told us that Don Carlos was not safe. There was something in the way the villagers looked at him and spoke of him that warned us: he was ceasing to be a man like other men, as an ox in the hands of the butcher ceases to be an ox for the herd. So the C—s stayed on though protesting every day, and the two boys went back every morning to feed the chickens. We did not much like their going, but we hoped they were safe, for they were hardly more than children and had been born in Chile and had Chilean papers. But the rest of the family never went out except into the garden, and after the first few days Don Carlos never left the house at all.

Then began a very strange period of our lives. Gradually we entered into a sort of region of nightmare; but it was a nightmare from which it was impossible to awake. We entered into it gradually, as I say, for though we were always apprehensive about Don Carlos, our anxiety at first was not very acute; and we genuinely enjoyed having them in the house; they were so attractive and pleasant to be with, and their devoted family life was a pleasure to watch. I never saw so happily attached a family. We were fortunate in being able to assume at first that Don Carlos and his family were with us only because of the danger of bombs falling on their house; that was a great advantage to us in the village because it was something everyone sympathised with. But as time went on and they did not go to their relations in Malaga, or move into some other house (a cousin, the Duquesa de — had a large empty house in the village where they had lived while their own house was being built the year before and where they could now have stayed most comfortably with all their chickens) – it became more and more difficult to pretend that they were only staying with us because of the air raids. The Village Committee had made it known to us through Enrique that they had nothing against Don Carlos. But not very long after that, a carpenter who had worked for us came in one evening and asked to see Gerald: what he had to tell him was that Don Carlos was 'wanted' by the Terrorists, and that they were looking for him in Malaga. After that we kept Don Carlos hidden, we did not say in so many words that he had gone, but if anyone asked about him on any particular day he was always said to be in Malaga then. He stayed upstairs where no one could see him; and we had a real hiding place, a very good one, a sort of priest's hole in which to hide him if the worst happened – uncertainty about the world in these modern days prevents me from telling where it was: we might want to use it again! As Doña Maria Louisa's mother, a charming old lady of seventy-six remarked to me one day, 'This reminds me so much of my youth, you know, when the Carlist Wars were going on.'

But even if we hid Don Carlos successfully, and we had worked out a plan with his family and with the servants of what we were all to do; particularly how the men who came for him were to be delayed while he got to his hiding place, which was the most difficult and uncertain part to manage – would not they take his young sons instead, even though they had Chilean papers? If they started to take his children we knew that Don Carlos, who was as brave as a lion anyway, would rush out and either get himself killed in a struggle or be taken off to Malaga, with the boys as well probably. Then, I must say that Gerald was something of a worry, too, to Enrique and me. He announced his intention of speaking to the men from the balcony if they came for Don Carlos, on the innocence of their proposed victim, and how ill such behaviour as theirs accorded with the pure Anarchist doctrine of the goodness of man, which needs no control.

Gerald is one of those people who, like the boy in the fairytale, have never learned to shiver and shake. It was a useful ignorance, I suppose, on the Western Front. But I must say that it has often been a highly agitating one to anyone who was fond of him. And there have been many occasions when I have wished that someone would bring the icy bucket full of fishes, and teach him to shiver and shake once and for all. I could not help admitting that his plan was worth trying; but I also could not help thinking that his frankness and fearlessness would make him say something tactless, and the end of it all would be a bullet through the head for him and the big door broken in and Don Carlos taken away.

There was an occasion on which Gerald tried to put his theory of reasoning with murderers into practice, not on behalf of Don Carlos, but of another friend of ours, Juan, the village baker. Juan was a charming man, honest, and a kind neighbour, and he was very popular in the village. But he was 'wanted' by the gangs in Malaga, because he was a devout Catholic and to the Right politically (though a sincere believer in some sort of social reform) and, most fatal of all, had acted as election agent for Gil Robles' Accion Catolica party in the elections some years before. Our village had nothing against him, he was known for his honesty and his kindness to his neighbours, particularly to the very poor. The Governor of Malaga gave him a safe conduct, all the political committees gave him safe conducts – and all of them were worthless, if one small band of murderous men chose to come for him.

Well, one day we heard that they had come. I was upstairs and heard a disturbance down the street, and went out on the balcony. The only thing I could see was Gerald striding rapidly down the street with his peculiar light springy walk. He was too far away to call, so I rushed downstairs and found Enrique very disturbed.

'Where has Don Geraldo gone?' I demanded.

'Gone to get himself killed by the Anarchists!' answered Enrique bitterly.

'But what is happening?'

'They've come for Juan.' I still remember only too clearly what I felt when Enrique said: *They've come for Juan.* The shock and horror of it, the pain I felt for Juan; and oddly enough the resignation and quietness of mind I felt about Gerald. I felt that he was doing what the circumstance and his nature demanded of him. He was obliged to try to save Juan from being murdered. If he were killed: still he had been right to attempt it. Fortunately as I reached that point in my thoughts and started down the street to find out what was happening, I saw him in the distance returning.

The gang had not come for Juan after all; but for a retired Civil Guard, who was said to have been unusually brutal and oppressive when he was in the force. And they were not going to murder him themselves, but take him into the prison in Malaga, and had now promised that he would be taken safely as far as the prison and delivered over to the proper authorities and they were allowing his wife and old mother to go with him as far as the prison door.

The village had violently opposed the demand for him. They said, as they always did in such cases, that Malaga had no right to take him, he was an *hijo del pueblo*, a son of the village – only the village knew his deeds and had the right to judge him. But the villagers had only a few old rifles, and the gang on the lorry were not only bristling with rifles and revolvers, but had a machine-gun which they trained on the villagers. Then unfortunately all the village Committee happened to be away so that there was no one in authority to oppose them. And in the end with menaces and threats of what the Terrorists would do to the village they got their way and carried him off. They were not one of the murder gangs who went about by night murdering people in the villages, where the country people would not do their duty as they said; but members of one of the 'Youth' organisations, and according to Gerald were a crew of hard-faced youths and girls. It was certainly a discouraging example of the activities of 'Youth' organisations, but one which was common I am told all over Spain on both sides and one which I should think would be observed anywhere where you had organisations of young irresponsible people and encouraged them to act for themselves against supposed enemies of the 'People' or the 'State' or whatever the popular watchword happened to be.

Gerald had given up his idea of addressing the gang when he saw how things were going; but he was so affected by what he had seen that he could not help making a speech about it to a large group of village men who had gathered around our door talking to Enrique. He told them how horrible it all was, how unworthy of human beings of any political persuasion. Finally he stopped and went in. Enrique followed us into the house and took me aside. 'For God's sake, stop Don Geraldo!' he said. 'He is going to get us all shot!' It seemed to me rather probable at the moment, for I could see that the villagers did not like his speech at all, and took it as a reflection on them and their ideas. And it was not a time to have differences with your neighbours. The villagers, it was true, killed no one themselves; but as someone put it to me, they sometimes 'threw the first stone'. For the people were beginning to change, as people do in wars. The change was largely due of course to the bombing, but also to the tales of executions and murders which refugees from the very beginning brought from the other side.

Poor Gerald, with his strong feelings of humanity and his tremendous energy, which made him feel that something should, and consequently must be done – and by him if there was no one else to do it, really suffered from the sensation of being powerless to help the people around him who were enduring so much from violence of all sorts, from the cruel night murders by the gangs of Terrorists and the terrifying bombing from the air.

He once proposed to beard the 'Committee of Public Safety' who, like the similarly named committee during the French Revolution, were supposed to decide who should be executed. (I do not think they did execute many people, the murders were the work of uncontrollable elements among the various parties or of mobs maddened by air raids.) 'But if I tell them what a dreadful impression these murders are creating abroad, surely they will try to stop them!' he said. Don Carlos was completely cynical as to the possibility of influencing such brutes as he said they must be. Doña Maria Louisa and I felt sure that whatever they were it would do no good, and that the attempt would be dangerous; the last thing we wanted was to attract attention to our household.

But Gerald did make one appeal of this sort one day when I was with him. We went to the office of the little Malaga newspaper, the only one that was still appearing, since the other presses had been burned in the fire. Before the rising it had been a moderately Left Wing little paper, but was now simply the voice of the times (it was in fact written in the usual war style familiar to most of us) – full of imaginary victories, talk about our heroic defenders who are conquering every-where, and about the 'cowardly *Fascistas*', who are unfortunately holding out to the death in a lot of places. This odd form of cowardice never seemed to strike them as peculiar, and the enemy were always automatically spoken of as 'cowardly *Fascistas*' even when they were described as holding some post until their last man had been killed.

We went to the office to make some enquiries: the editor excused himself, but sent out a young assistant. We asked the young man if something could not be done by appeals to the public in the press to stop the murders. He rather tried to make light of it all, admitting that there were a few unfortunately unavoidable incidents; but 'You mustn't dwell on the disagreeable side of Revolutions,' which angered us very much. But he had in spite of his words a troubled look, and I think did both fear and hate what was going on, though he probably naturally resented having suggestions made to him by two unknown foreigners.

I must say our conduct did remind me a little of George Fox, when as an obscure and proscribed Quaker he describes himself as telling everyone their duty, 'Just then I felt moved to write to the King to reprove his conduct towards the dissenters.'

Both then and later every organisation, Anarchist, Communist, Socialist and Republican alike, condemned and deplored the killings. I remember seeing Malaga plastered with posters by the Anarchists calling on the wilder elements among them to cease their brutalities which were disgracing the whole organisation and shaming them in the eyes of the world. But I do not believe that there was even one murder the fewer for all their fervent words. And this nightly murdering went on getting worse and worse until for a week or so there was a veritable reign of terror. People were even dragged out of hotels in the centre of Malaga. There was no protection for them. It was appalling.

Then suddenly one day when we went in to Malaga we found nearly all the red flags gone. Republican flags and streamers had taken their place. Everyone seemed more cheerful, and we wondered what could have happened. The story which we heard from various quarters was that the Militia and the Assault Guards (a body formed by the Republic and generally loyal to it) had declared that they would cease fighting and lay down their arms unless the murdering ceased. They said that they would not fight to defend a community of assassins. As together they were practically the entire fighting force their defection would have been fatal, so that their declaration had a great effect, especially as it coincided with strong representations from Madrid on the harm their violence was doing the Government cause both at home and abroad. For some time the murders almost ceased and they were never resumed in the same way. The centre of Malaga became fairly safe for the suspected and 'wanted' even at night. Guards were stationed at the doors of the hotels, and all doors were ordered shut and locked at night, and only to be opened to Militia who showed a proper authority from the Governor.

The murders never became so bad again, as I have said, but they continued slowly getting worse as the effect of the various declarations wore off. It would surely have been possible to stop them if there had been a comparatively small body of energetic and determined men of forceful character who were bent upon doing so.* But with great natural energy the Spanish often combine a strange apathy, an inability to act at some crucial moment. It has often betrayed them in their wars.

It must have been examples of this apathy, this strange, sometimes fatal, inertia, as well as his observation of their wonderful stoicism and heroic patience (how often shown in these days!) which made General Napier in his History of the Peninsular War pronounce his odd judgement upon the Spanish – which, while I feel it to be a libel upon one of the noblest races, always amuses me in spite of myself by its oddity and by some essential truth of caricature in it.

'The Spaniards,' he said, 'are a race of many virtues, but unfortunately their virtues are passive and their faults are active.'

---

* An acute and disinterested observer, a well-known journalist, who visited Malaga not long before it was taken, tells me that it was then perfectly orderly. The people were sunk in a sort of stoical misery due to the incessant and horrible bombing and shelling from the sea, and hunger and fear of the Nationalists at their gates. (He says he hardly saw a smile.) But the murder gangs had been put down and the prisoners were safe. It is what I would expect of the Spanish people that under any conditions, however horrible, their natural humanity would assert itself.

Chapter 10

THERE IS A VERY CURIOUS and uncomfortable feeling about living among uncontrolled human beings. I used to feel it particularly sometimes when we were coming back on the train from Malaga. I felt that it was like being surrounded by a herd of buffaloes or a pack of wild dogs, or I suppose like living among savages on some remote island. The crowds were good humoured and friendly: it seemed as if there were nothing to be afraid of. But you were dependent on their changing humour: if it grew dangerous, there was no power to control them – and I am not a pure Anarchist to believe in man's perfect natural goodness. Not that I thought the Spanish people naturally bad, but like all crowds capricious and easily swayed.

I was not exactly afraid myself to be among them; I never believed that English people were in danger in 'Red Spain' in spite of some of the consuls. But I was afraid simply of what might happen around me, of being involved as a witness in some movement of mob violence. But the crowds on trains and buses were actually as good humoured and good mannered as ever. Once I did see two old men taken off the train. They were priests who had tried to get away to Malaga dressed in ordinary clothes, but had been recognised and given away by some one on the train. When it stopped at the next station some members of the local committee were waiting, and the two poor old men were taken off, but without any manifestation of anything except curiosity, everyone craning out of windows to see what was happening. The priests were politely helped into a waiting car, and taken off to the prison in Malaga for 'safe keeping'. Unfortunately it was not a very safe prison to be in. People were taken out and shot after every bad air raid. It was the same on both sides judging by accounts given us later by Italian journalists who had been in Nationalist Spain. Their accounts of what happened there were almost indistinguishable from accounts of what happened in Malaga.

Hate rises very high during air raids, especially raids at night. These droning aeroplanes like searching bees seem seeking out everyone's hiding place. Peasants cannot feel (could any of us?) that the bomb which killed little three year old Mariquilla and mangled little José fell on those two children by pure chance and was really meant to destroy an ammunition dump. They think, and rightly, that when you drop bombs from a great height, almost at random from thousands of feet up, you are to blame when they fall on women, children, old people, the wounded, the sick. The aviator above seeking for a place to sow destruction seems like a peering devil. The bomb falls, kills its innocent victims: the angry people must be paid blood for blood. The quarter rises and goes off to the prison, and there is another murder of forty or fifty or a hundred poor people, most of them as innocent as the slaughtered children. And I believe that far from being peculiar to Spain, the same thing will happen wherever you have air raids and there are any prisoners of war or other helpless unfortunates the mob can revenge itself upon.

I did have a rather horrid experience one day on the road to Malaga, but not in a train or bus. We had particularly wanted to go in early one morning, but found when we got down to the square that the ancient bus had broken down completely; so we started walking along the road hoping that some lorry would come along and offer us a lift, but nothing did come, and we finally reached the main road to Algeçiras. As we were already extremely hot and tired and Malaga still many miles away, we stopped in the shade of a eucalyptus tree where a countryman and his wife were standing, and opened the usual conversation with them. They said that probably the Torremolinos bus would come if we waited long enough. They had apparently been waiting for hours, but they had the usual patience of the Spanish poor and we had not. However it was so hot that we waited with them and presently an empty lorry came along and offered us a lift.

Gerald and the countryman got in behind and the woman and I, as señoras, were invited to get up in front. I sat next to the driver, and was much annoyed because he began to press against me and stroke my leg. I have often been pressed and stroked in crowded buses and trains by strangers in Spain; and, sitting down alone for a minute to wait for someone in Malaga cafés have become the centre of a sort of Mad Hatter's tea-party of men who sit down at my table and silently stare with fixed and glassy eyes, like Mock Turtles. (I should explain that this is peculiar to the south of Spain where respectable women do not go to cafés alone.)

But the villagers and workmen had never behaved like that (perhaps only because the English seem such a different race that they appear no more desirable than zebras or hornbuck); and I was particularly annoyed by the lorry driver's approaches because they were so openly made in the presence of another respectable woman, and also for the perhaps rather odd reason that I felt that he was behaving badly in time of revolution. I felt that all restraint being removed, he should have restrained himself.

But his attention was suddenly called away from me and he began to grin with simple pleasure and cry 'Look! Look!' pointing to the side of the road and almost stopping the lorry in his eagerness to see something better.

I looked and saw the body of a dead man lying beside the road. It was the body of a large old man dressed in trousers and a white shirt, and it lay on its back with one hand thrown over the head and the other still clasping the torn stomach. The face was glazed with blood and the shirt was almost crimson with it. The thing that was lying there seemed too large and stiff ever to have been a man. It looked like a large dirty doll someone had thrown away. I only saw the body for a minute, but in that minute I had a very intense and curious impression – I not only knew that what I saw was not alive, I knew that it *never had been alive*. That thing I saw lying beside the road was a castaway mechanical doll, a broken automaton, nothing more. It never had been anything more.

One day late in August when it was even hotter than usual, Pilar and Enrique had been to Malaga to try to buy some coffee and tins of meat or fish. Food was getting short – the shops would only sell a small quantity of each article to each customer. Tinned foods had almost disappeared, cheese had vanished completely, even *bacalao* (dried salt cod), that stand-by of the poor kitchen, was getting very scarce. The last time I had been to Malaga I had bought one of these flat ill-smelling fish; but the shopkeeper had said sadly, 'It is the last I can let you have, Señora; there are no more than a dozen left in the storehouse. I don't know what is going to happen.' I thoroughly appreciated the serious-ness of a shortage of *bacalao*, highly nourishing as it is, and each smallest piece capable of giving a queer flavour to whole cauldrons of rice or soup; though nothing will ever make me resigned to its taste or smell, reminiscent, as one of our unfortunate guests in the old days in the sierra put it, of 'feeding time in the Lion house'.

But it is the food of foods to the poor – when there is no cheap fish to be had, when the weather is so bad that the fishing-boats do not go out, and there are no sardines and *boquerones* to be bought, there is always *bacalao*. It is cheap and a very little goes a long way; and whole families who never taste meat get warmth and nourishment from their stew flavoured with small bits of it. And I began that day really to worry about food – not for ourselves, we could manage I thought until we somehow contrived to get our refugees out of the country, or until

Malaga was taken and they ceased to be dependent on us. Even in famines you can generally buy something if you have the money, and we hoped always to be able to get that somehow from Gibraltar – but what would the poor do when bread was scarce and *bacalao* gone? They could not live on tomatoes and French beans, which was all our garden, for instance, was producing late in August.

Enrique was counting the days until he could put in his potatoes, and he meant to plant as large a crop as possible: all the land we had available was to be in potatoes and beans. For Enrique expected hunger; he had seen hunger before and saw it coming now. No one was cultivating the land, no one was preparing for their winter crops.

'They are going to be hungrier than the cats this winter!' he kept saying, an extremely telling expression in Spain where poor pussy always goes hungry.

That day in the hot and dusty end of August it was getting late, and I was beginning to look out anxiously for Pilar and Enrique – we were always anxious if anyone was out of sight for long in those days. Finally I saw them coming slowly down the street looking hot and tired, and went down to the kitchen to greet them and hear any news. Pilar took a whole kilo of coffee out of her basket, two kilos of sugar, and a great pile, almost an arroba, of russet ripe muscatels. It was far more than I had expected them to get, and I was much pleased; but they both seemed sad and discouraged even beyond the habit of the time.

'What's the matter?' I asked.

'Those people of Malaga!' said Enrique in a tone of fastidious disgust.

'What happened?' I asked. It was evidently something painful.

'Well,' said Enrique, 'we were in a narrow street somewhere above the Calle San Juan – I can't tell just where it was, Malaga is so vast a capital! when we saw a crowd about someone or something at the door of a house. We thought someone was hurt so we went to see; but it was not that –'

'What was it then?'

'It was a poor old priest who had come in from the country in disguise and tried to hide himself in some friends' house, and some one had given him away, and a mob had come after him. They were mostly women – Señora, *que caffres!* What kaffirs! They were beating the poor old man and trying to kick him only there were so many trying to get at him that most of them couldn't reach him. But the women were the worst; they hit him on the head and spit in his face and some of them blew their noses on his cape. I never saw anything so ugly – '

'What happened to him?' I asked, sickened by the picture I imagined. 'Was he killed?'

'No,' said Enrique, *'Gracias a Dios!* a Guardia de Asalto came and said he would shoot the next man or woman who touched him, and he took the poor creature off to prison all covered with dirt and blood.' *Where he'll be shot after the next air raid*, I thought. Anyway he will probably have a quiet, quick death. It is the best you can hope for in a civil war if you are on the wrong side – to be killed as quickly and painlessly as possible, as early in the day as you can manage it.

'Que caffres! que caffres!' Enrique kept repeating.

After the bombing began the atmosphere had grown steadily worse. It is inevitable where open towns are bombed. Hate is the other side of fear. And it was horrible to see and feel this wave of hate-fear rising around us like a menacing sea. The talk of the villagers came to be more and more about *Fascistas*, and the *Fascista* was a purely mythical creature of unimaginable wickedness (twin brother I should think to the 'Red' of some of our daily papers) always mentioned in a special tone of horror. There was of course a great deal of talk about atrocities the *Fascistas* were committing; but also (a most curious feature of the war mentality) a good deal about atrocities they were supposed to be committing themselves, many of them quite imaginary. For instance

I was told a melodramatic story about a hunt for a *Fascista* which had taken place near us, and how they had fired the cane brake to burn him out. 'That men should hunt each other like beasts!' they added in enjoyment of horror. But the whole story was quite fantastic. The hunt had never happened. The cane brakes were always catching fire in dry weather from the sparks from the train which ran through them at that point, and the sight of the blackened field had suggested the whole story to the atrocity making instinct.

I was struck by what I can only call a look of dreamy blood-lust upon their faces as they told such stories. I realised then, what I realised even more clearly later at Gibraltar, listening to the English talk of atrocities, what atrocity stories really are: they are the pornography of violence. The dreamy lustful look that accompanies them, the full enjoyment of horror (especially noticeable in respectable elderly Englishmen speaking of the rape or torture of naked nuns: it is significant that they are always *naked* in such stories), show only too plainly their erotic source.

I do not claim of course that no atrocities have been committed in Spain: I am sure they have been. Or even that there were not isolated cases in the Great War. War often produces atrocities. But more than ninety-nine hundredths of all atrocity stories, are, I am sure, always products of the diseased and perverse imagination.

I don't believe that anyone entirely escapes the evil influences of war. Enrique was a most sensitive and peaceful young man, and the ugly scene he saw in Malaga appalled him. And yet even in Enrique I noticed a change. The evil in the air was corrupting everybody. It is the same in all wars, a contagious delirium rises from the spilled blood and infects everyone with its ugly madness. I was talking to Enrique in the garden one evening not long after that day, when he began to tell me a story about a man he knew of who had joined one of the murder gangs. He had heard that his brother-in-law had been killed in Seville, and was throwing himself into the work of revenge.

'He says that two hundred Fascists must die to revenge his brother-in-law!' Enrique said, with a sort of dreamy lustful enjoyment that absolutely amazed me. I was about to protest that nobody's brother-in-law was sufficient excuse for murdering two hundred people, most of them probably innocent of having done anything at all; but old Maria was before me.

'*Deben de matarle enseguida!*' she said severely – 'They ought to kill *him* at once!' Enrique was silenced, and picking up his tools went quietly to work among his flowers. When I say that everyone was corrupted, I ought to except Maria: I do not think she was ever affected at all. Her disapproval of all these goings on of Left and Right only became deeper and deeper every day. She snorted when she spoke of 'these *Anarchistas!*' She breathed fire when she spoke of 'these *Fascistas!*' Everything that interrupted the natural order of things, of birth and burial, sowing and harvest, was evil as a matter of course to her, and should be stopped as soon as possible. All these newfangled ideas were ruining the country. We should all suffer for the folly and presumption of misguided men – but not, on her part at least, suffer in silence! She was always indignant, and as she was unable to catch the Fascists and Anarchists and give them a piece of her mind, we all suffered for it, and Pilar grew wanner than ever.

But I used to feel sometimes – and with comfort – that Maria was perhaps after all the real voice of Spain, and that when all this delirium was over, Maria and her kind would still be found saying: 'Let us have no *novedad*! None of your nonsense!' And we would all sigh with relief and go back to the austere hard-working life of peace.

'I am for that party,' Enrique once said, 'who let me cultivate my cabbages.'

Chapter *11*

SOME OF MY MOST vivid impressions of that time are of scenes
and encounters against a background of crowded cafés or noisy
streets. Of enemy aeroplanes over Malaga, and the militia and workmen rushing out into the streets, asking 'Are they ours?' 'Are they the
Fascists?' Then the crash of the first bomb falling and a fusillade of
pistol shots from the excited crowds trying in vain to hit these birds
of prey – and often someone wounded or killed by stray bullets. Of
soldiers' funerals passing by followed by fellow trades unionists, sad
old men and women in dusty black, and wondering children. Of
untrained boys going off to the front in lorries, shouting, singing,
waving to the crowds in the street, who seemed to look after them
with more pity than enthusiasm, saluting, calling goodbye, *Salud!*
Salud!

One chance meeting I remember with two of the political exiles
occurred (modern life is always producing these unsuitable conjunc-
tions!) in an ice-cream parlour – of all places to be sitting in during a
revolution with the smoke of burning buildings in the air. However,
there we were sitting, for it was in the early days when the cafés and
restaurants were still closed. The 'ice-cream parlour' as it sold only
cooling ices was allowed to open first.

We found it open with delight and were sitting eating lemon-water
ices and drinking *chufa*, that queer thick whitish drink made of the
roots of irises which Spaniards love. The ices were rather expensive,
the cheapest cost threepence, far too dear for the Spanish poor, and in

those days there were very few of the well-to-do about, so that the 'parlour' though it was the only place of refreshment open, was not crowded. As we sat enjoying the contrast of our cool drinks in the shade with the heat and glare of the street outside, some foreigners we had seen in Torremolinos passed by, so we spoke to them and asked them to come in and have something with us.

They were a married couple, he a Pole and she a German, and they were exiles for their beliefs. I remember how the Pole stretched out his hands in a gesture of despair over the situation in Spain, and the hopeless, disillusioned look on his face as he said: 'I have been through five revolutions, and the state of the country was always worse afterwards than before.' We asked him naturally if he had been through the Russian Revolution, but he had missed this greatest one; his had been obscure sad struggles which made no particular stir in the indifferent world.

Later on the same couple very kindly tried to help us. They somehow heard of the difficulties we were having trying to save Don Carlos and get him out of the country, and came over from Torremolinos to tell us that it was possible to buy forged Danish passports for twenty-five pounds (why Danish of all things?), or Polish nationality papers for five pounds. We would have somehow raised the money and got the Danish passport for Don Carlos; but when we told him about it he said that it was no use. Everyone in Spain knows everyone else: some of the officials on the docks would have been sure to recognise him; and that of course would have been fatal, he would have been taken straight to prison and only left it in all probability to meet a firing squad.

It was remarkable how freely we ourselves moved about all the time during the Civil War. We went everywhere we wanted to, took long walks in the country, and went all over Malaga; and while we did carry our passports when we remembered to I do not think we were ever asked for them. I only remember one occasion when we really aroused suspicion. We had been sitting drinking tea one afternoon at the English Club, when we suddenly realised that our bus would be leaving in five minutes, so we hurriedly jumped up and ran down the stairs and out into the street. The sidewalks and the park were crowded and there was a sudden movement towards us and a rising murmur of 'Fascists!' Then some of them recognised us – there were so few foreigners in Malaga at that time that they were all known by sight – and someone said 'Oh! It's only those English,' and everyone drifted away again. It was only the foolish innocent English, no harm in them.

I remember another chance meeting we had in a café with an old friend who had done some work for us. He was a very clever craftsman, not a Malagueñan but from somewhere in the north. To our surprise he turned out to be an important leader among the Anarcho-Syndicalists. He was an intelligent, humane man, and deplored the murders as we did, and we kept urging him that day to try to use any influence he had to stop such things. But he sat looking beyond our day into that Future World of the Idealist. Soon – very soon now! – Man would be Free – Man would be Good – Man would be Happy. I looked at him sadly as he sat drinking his coffee and smiling at us from under his thatch of white hair with happy shining eyes – looked at him with sympathy and with pity as one might look at a dreaming youth, whose radiant dreams are destined never to be fulfilled in this world.

Another café meeting of that time still affects me painfully. It was with a Russian – not one of the 'Russian Agitators' about whom we used to hear so much in Gibraltar, but a White Russian, a refugee from the Russian Revolution. We knew him well because he had become a chauffeur and now owned his own car, and had often driven us, and had also formerly acted as chauffeur to friends of ours. Just before the trouble began he had exchanged his Nansen passport for Spanish papers, which he had bought for some quite small sum; but now regretted the exchange. He had just joined the Syndicalist trades union in the faint hope of saving his car from being commandeered as it was all he had to get his living by. So far he had succeeded, but he told us that he did not think it would be possible for him to keep it much longer.

But what I remember so painfully about the meeting is the state of fear that he was in. He would talk nothing but English which he had learned at school in Russia and spoke very badly; his face was white and drawn, and his dark restless eyes were never still, turning constantly from side to side, anxiously examining the faces around him. Was he simply terrified (I wondered) at finding himself in the midst of a Revolution again, like the one which had destroyed his home and turned him into an exile? Was it possible (I do not know why I should have thought of this) that he could be acting as a spy for the Nationalists? Could that be why he was so afraid? This idea which came to me even then while I watched his white face and restless eyes, had a curious half-confirmation later. We were told that in an empty house which we knew he often visited because he had once worked there and was friendly with the caretakers, the military experts had discovered a Nationalists' sending station. However, he was not arrested then or later; so I think either that he had nothing to do with it, or (even more likely), that the whole story was the usual baseless fabrication.

It does not matter what I write about him now, for he is dead. He was accidentally killed (such are the accidents of war!) in the hospital in Malaga, where he was lying ill with bronchitis. A bomb fell on the ward and wrecked it. Poor Pedro, I do not like to think of his death, but I like even less to think of the long-drawn-out terrors that preceded it.

One of these chance café meetings led to our spending a very unpleasant night. We were sitting drinking tea in what remained of the Café E— (part of it had been destroyed) when we noticed that a young man who had sat down at a table near us was unmistakably

English. He was extremely young with blond close-clipped curly hair and a childish, chubby face. We naturally spoke to him and discovered to our surprise that he was one of our 'War Correspondents', representing in fact one of our largest popular dailies. He must have been somewhat hampered in this career, we could not help thinking, by the fact that he was practically a child, had never seen a shot fired in anger (as he kept complaining) – and spoke no Spanish. He had not even managed to see any atrocities as yet, though that, we gathered, was what was chiefly expected of him.

We tried to encourage him by telling him that if he spent a day or two in Malaga he was sure to see some bombing at any rate. Finally we agreed to have dinner with him at his hotel and try to tell him something about the war. He had been in the north and should have known more about it than we did; but his lack of Spanish and entire ignorance about Spain had prevented him from learning anything worth knowing.

The full moon was rising we noticed as we left the café, but somehow the significance of that failed to impress us; for up till then we had never been raided at night, but always in the day or just at dawn. We would miss the last bus back by staying to dinner, but everything was fairly normal at the moment and there were taxis for hire. Don Carlos was not with us then, or of course we would not have stayed away from home at night.

We enjoyed the dinner which was much better than anything we could get at that time; and after it when we were drinking our coffee in the glassed-in patio we spread out a map of Spain on the table and tried to show this 'War Correspondent' where the lines probably were. The waiters in Spanish style leaning over our shoulders and arguing the point with the greatest animation and friendliness. An armed patrol which came in for their free supper and saw what we were doing only grinned at us and saluted.

Suddenly the lights went out. There were startled exclamations, and then listening silence – and in the silence we could hear the drone of an aeroplane – aeroplanes – coming closer, hovering overhead, searching like bees, and then the crash of the first bomb.

'My God!' said Gerald. 'That's a real bomb at last, a two hundred kilo, I should think.' Another bomb shattered the silence with its horrible rending crash, and with the crash there was a chorus of shrill cries, and the cries seemed to me to be dragged down by the roaring crash of the bomb, and carried down with it through the earth.

Looking up we could see the moon shining in through the glass roof above us, and I thought rather absurdly: *People who live in glass houses shouldn't throw stones.* We withdrew to the stairs which seemed a little safer, though the Hotel I— had not been built with bombs in mind. The crashes came again and again, but further away each time, over the port. Gradually the droning died away and finally ceased: the raiders were gone.

We went out to the street door but we found that a horrible change had come over the city. The friendly waiters glared at us suspiciously – for all they knew we might have been signalling to the enemy with night-lights (a charge seriously made against a Spanish woman I knew). Armed patrols were dashing up and down the street in motor-cars, trying to find out in the darkness and confusion where the damage was. We persuaded one of them to take along our young journalist, anxious to see some bloody bodies. I thought he was brave, for the patrol with their waving revolvers and angry excited speech which he could not understand did not seem safe companions for a moonlight ride.

We had seen enough, and only wanted to go home; but there were no taxis and if there had been it would not have been safe to take one as we would probably have been shot by some nervous patrol for fleeing Fascists; so we asked for a room for the night. The manager and the waiters would hardly answer, staring at us with angry, frightened, suspicious eyes. An old chambermaid finally took us up to a room sighing as she went: '*Ay, mi Madre!*' and occasionally whispering an invocation to the Virgin. But she at least was not full of hate, but only sadly resigned to these inexplicable horrors, and regarded us merely as poor fellow sufferers, all of us likely to be killed together before the night was over.

The room they gave us had two enormous glass windows on to the street. There were no mosquito nets, and the droning of the mosquitoes was incessant. I had given up all idea of sleeping and was consequently falling into a doze when it seemed to me that the mosquitoes' note was changing. Then came the familiar crash of a fallen bomb. We jumped up and went into the bathroom to escape the glass windows, and looking up again perceived the moonlight shining down on us through a glass skylight.

'Good Lord! what is this place?' said Gerald in disgust. 'The Crystal Palace?' 'I shall stay here,' I answered tiredly. 'There aren't so many mosquitoes anyway.'

The raid was soon over; but it was impossible to sleep again for the town was horribly awake. An armed gang was going about dragging people 'on the Right' out of their houses. There were thundering knockings, cries of 'Bring out the Fascists!', women's screams. We lay awake, feeling with horror the tide of fear-hate rising around us, knowing what would happen before the night was over – the murder of prisoners by the fear-maddened mob. And this not because the mob was one of Spaniards as we are so fond of saying: it will happen in England if there are any prisoners to murder unless the police are too strong for the crowd: it will happen in any city where there are air raids. It is the answer fear makes to its enemies. Indeed, something like it almost happened during the Great War when they paraded the German prisoners on the coast after one of the Zeppelin raids. Only the determination of the soldiers and police saved the prisoners from injury. Soldiers who were there still speak of the mob's behaviour with horror.

During the night there were two more raids; but one raid is much like another unless they are using really big bombs, and they fall close to you; then they are really appalling and unforgettable. The next morning the day dawned as brilliant and cloudless as if the dark night had never been. But the whole city seemed different to us. The hotel-keeper and the waiters no longer seemed suspicious but sullen and ashamed and only anxious to get rid of us, and we felt that we never wanted to see them again. Everyone seemed tarred with the same brush, stained with the same foulness of mania and crime.

We escaped thankfully from the hotel and went to the café for our coffee and rolls and met there our young journalist sitting over his. He was full of gratitude – thanks to us he had seen a shockingly wounded man and two horribly mangled dead women in a house which had been wrecked by a bomb. He had also been to the cemetery that morning to see the bodies of the prisoners who had been shot at dawn. The bodies were piled in a trench, forty of them, he said. But we noticed that by an ingenious system known to atrocity collectors he seemed to have multiplied the number by four in his story which he showed us.

But he was really a very nice boy, and he seemed sick and unable to eat as he told us about the bodies lying uncovered in a long trench so that people could go in and have a look at them. And he had acquired overnight a new trick of staring apprehensively at the faces around him. I think that everyone in Malaga that morning felt dislike and distrust of his fellow men. It was like the morning after some debauch, when people feel that they have been taking part in something ugly and feel sullen and ashamed.

A window in the café had been shattered by the wind of an explosion near it, and I thought again absurdly – *People who live in glass houses shouldn't throw stones.* Just then a nervous waiter dropped a tray full of tumblers at our feet, and we and everyone else in the café leaped into the air.

'Let's go before anything else gets broken,' Gerald said. Outside the street still smelled like burnt-out grates when we stopped at the corner to say goodbye to the young journalist. He seemed to me rather pathetically like a brave boy who had wandered into the wrong world, and I hoped that he would go home soon to the England of gardens and policemen before anything happened to him.

When we got back to the village at last we found the servants in tears – they were sure that we had been killed by a bomb.

One last memory of that time – not ugly but only sad. I have not mentioned Pilar's gentle timid romance for a long time. I have not spoken of it because it was over so soon. Her one fair day had ended almost as soon as it began.

One morning a fortnight or so after Don Carlos came to us Pilar put on a new dress she had just had made from some cheap silk I had given her. I think there is something very touching in the fact that there is a special word in Spanish for the first wearing of a new garment: it shows how few new clothes most Spaniards ever have. The word is *estrenar* and that morning Pilar was *estrenaring* her new dress, and we were all teasing her about it.

'*Que guapa está Pilar estrenando todos los dias un trajo nuevo!*'
'*Ya que tiene novio – !*'

Pilar, wearing an air of ironic indifference, was secretly much pleased by our teasing and by being again after so many barren lonely years in the position of a girl with a *novio*, a *prétendant*, and a new dress to wear for him. She had even stuck a scarlet hibiscus flower in the knot of her long black hair, and I thought, looked really beautiful, the flaming passionate red of the great wide flower contrasting so strangely with her thin dark face of a melancholy resigned Madonna.

Gerald and I had to go to Malaga and hurried off after lunch, leaving Pilar serving coffee to the C — s in the upstairs *sala* where they generally sat in order to be with Don Carlos. I heard her laughing at some joke as we went down the street.

We got back late in the afternoon. There seemed to be an unusual number of people in the street, and I thought that they looked at us strangely. I was filled with alarm for our refugees – could the Terrorists have come for Don Carlos while we were away? We hurried on. As we entered the stable we heard a babble of high voices in the kitchen and hurried more. When we entered we saw our usual old women in a state of excitement and distress. Pilar sat quietly weeping in a corner, and even old Maria seemed sad and disturbed.

Antonio had been killed. He had been talking to a friend in the street who was as unused to firearms as he was himself. The friend, telling some exciting story, made a careless gesture and his gun went off shooting Antonio through the heart and killing him instantly. We had been right in thinking that the villagers looked at us in a particular way. They had been silently commiserating with us on the misfortune that had befallen our house.

I do not think that Pilar had ever been at all in love with Antonio: he was really a very dull young man. But his attachment had been the greatest pleasure of her life. And it had given her dignity and value in her own eyes. It had been a late, thin blooming after barren lonely years. And now it was over.

Everyone was much shocked and grieved by poor Antonio's death – for what had that poor, good young man to do with war? Poor as he was he had had one proud possession with which to endow Pilar if she would have him as well as his strength and willingness to work – if only there were any work. It was, like Maria of Cártama's olive trees, a small but on that account all the more dearly valued possession. It was in fact a little patch of ground near his village, about a quarter of an acre of unirrigated *secano* with two old carob trees growing on it and half a dozen young olives of his own planting which would not bear for years to come.

Late that night when all the neighbours had gone, Pilar came to my room where I was undressing. She had a dirty crumpled piece of paper in her hand. It was Antonio's will carefully written out by himself and found in his breast pocket after his death.

'Oh! Señora,' she said, and her voice moved me with its grief and pity for the dead young man.

'Señora, he left me his olive trees – ' and she threw herself weeping in my arms.

Chapter 12

I T IS EASY TO IMAGINE how much this reign of terror worried us for the safety of Don Carlos and his family. We had come to identify ourselves with them and with their fate. We felt that we *must* save him. It was as if we had been chosen by fate or providence to protect them in their danger. Much as I liked and admired Don Carlos, it was as much for the sake of the family happiness as anything else that I so wanted to save him. They were so charming as a family and so happy together. There would have been something so truly horrible in this mutual love and happiness being shattered by a brutal murder, and the wife and children left desolate.

I cannot speak too highly of Don Carlos's courage and of his wonderful gaiety and good humour in the horrible position in which he found himself, when he must have felt like a rabbit in a burrow when the weasels are sniffing about the entrance eager for its blood – and how much more poignantly, since we have been given these too-tightly drawn nerves, this too-lively imagination as if it were to enable us to suffer as intensely as possible the apprehension of approaching evil.

I think it was really remarkable that far from being sad or silent we used often to have the gayest evenings – a hush falling only when we heard a lorry stopping outside, then some of us would creep to the windows on the street anxiously watching what the armed men in the lorry would do. When we saw that they had only come to change the patrol, and the lorry began to move off again, we would all give a long breath of relief, and come back to our seats, rather thoughtful for a while until the indomitable Don Carlos would make some joke or begin some amusing story.

But over our bean stew or whatever it was that Maria had managed to get for us that day, and our pint of wine between the eight of us, brought in secret from the shop by Pilar hidden in her basket or apron, we used often to talk and laugh until the servants would tell us we were making too much noise, the villagers in the kitchen would disapprove of our hilarity in these times.

Don Carlos had an endless fund of amusing stories. One I remember, which diverted me extremely was a description of a curious reform school run by the Brothers of some teaching order for the obstreperous sons of the rich, who had, I suppose, been spoiled by their too indulgent Spanish parents. The boys were extremely tough, but the Brothers were tougher and went about armed with life-preservers. A boy began to make trouble – BAM!!!! as the comic strips say, a Brother landed him one on the side of the head, and when he recovered consciousness the lesson continued. According to Don Carlos the school had a notable success and some famous alumni, one of whom, a friend of his, had given him a striking description of the course of his studies.

Another of Don Carlos's stories amused us very much, I remember, as a tale of the times. A cousin of his, a gentle rather timid young man, had to go from one house to another during the first days of the rising. He was frightened of the journey because his way lay partly along the main road; but all went well until he met one of the usual lorries full of armed men who all greeted him with shouts of *Salud!* and enthusiastically saluted with thrown-up arms. He timidly returned the salute as best he could – when to his horror, the lorry pulled up with a great grinding of brakes and several heavily armed men got out. He was paralysed with fear but determined to die bravely. The leader, a perfect walking arsenal, came up to him – he waited for the shot or blow that was to end it all – then the leader said in good humoured reproof: 'That's not the way – you've got it all wrong! It's the *left* arm. It's not meant for a menace: it's a greeting, a salute – see, like this!' and he threw up his arm in the correctly made Popular Front salute.

It was later at night when we went to bed that the real horror of the situation which we had been keeping away with talk and laughter would flow back upon us. Then, when the lights were out and the old house dark and silent, fear would come out of the darkness. Then I used to lie awake listening for the coming of the murderers. And those hours had exactly the quality of a nightmare – the feeling that something horrible was coming – the inability to flee – the inability to wake –

I used to think then, and I still think with absolute horror of what the people of Spain have suffered: of the nightmare life which thousands and thousands of people on both sides have led, until at last the hiding place was discovered – and there was the knocking at the door, and the voice of their enemies at last –

We used to listen, as I say, for the coming of the murderers – and once we heard them come – but not thank Heaven! to us. We heard lorries down in the village below, shouts, cries, protests, loud knockings on a door, angry voices, women's agonised screams. We lay awake wondering for whom they had come, what was happening in the darkness below us, whether they would come to us. Then at last the lorries went away, the angry, troubled voices died down, even the last sound, a woman's sobbing, died away, and a brooding silence lay over the houses.

The next morning we learned for whom they had come; and the next afternoon we met a small procession of men going to the cemetery carrying on their shoulders the cheap coffin containing the body of the poor man who had been shot, recovered from some field or ditch. The men of the village who walked with the body had troubled, sullen faces.

The people of Malaga had done this thing against their wills. The dead man had been an *hijo del pueblo*, a son of the village, whatever his faults, and the village alone had had the right to judge him. They had tried, and been unable, to protect him, and they felt wronged and insulted by his death. The solidarity of village life, the most important unity in their lives, had been broken.

Don Carlos's courage and good spirits in his terrible situation were really beyond praise, and so indeed was the behaviour of the whole family. Doña Maria Louisa was in any case almost a saint, one of those lovely, practical Spanish saints. She used generally to sit up all night, so that Don Carlos could sleep tranquilly knowing that someone was always on the watch, and also so that she would be dressed and ready if the worst did happen. How many times I remember getting up myself in the night at that time hearing a car stop nearby, creeping silently to the window and looking cautiously out. Feeling all the time that I would have been much better in bed. After all if the Terrorists came we should soon know it! (I had the same feeling about air raids but much more strongly. There is no danger of sleeping through an air raid, and the possibility that there might be one never kept us awake for a minute.) The house was fortunately a perfect fortress like all old country houses in Spain; the windows barred with iron *rejas* and tremendous bars of iron carried across the outside doors (the one on the street door was so heavy that Maria could hardly lift it into place). There was no question of anyone entering the house except with a battering ram unless we opened the door to them ourselves, and that was going to give us time to prepare for them.

Actually we were much safer at night than in the day when the open stable door into which anyone could come (though they could only get to the house by going through the kitchen wing where Maria was generally lying in wait for them), was an unavoidable danger, since to shut it against the constant stream of visitors and hucksters would have aroused too much suspicion.

For we still had visitors all day, but now only our old women came and a few near neighbours with young children who were more afraid of going to the sierra than of staying in our house. Most of our village friends had fallen away. It was not that they had ceased to be our friends, but because they were afraid to come near Don Carlos. As someone says *The condemned are contagious*, and we too carried something of the infection about us. Our richer village friends, the farmers, bailiffs, master masons, people of mildly conservative sympathies and consequently apt to be suspect, never came at all, though they sent us messages by Enrique. It was as if we had a case of smallpox in the house.

I think that it was only our chorus of old women who never seemed to think of us as being infectious at all. A great deal of the 'character' for which the Spanish are famous I think is found most of all in its older women. They have suffered and resigned themselves, worked beyond their strength, spent themselves for others. This patient stoicism, a stoicism that is not hard, but gentle and quietly resigned, accepting life as it is with all its ills and griefs with dignity and without complaint, is one of the most remarkable of Spanish characteristics. And it has been seen a thousand times everywhere in Spain during this war.

Napier has a story which I think illustrates it very well of something he saw when he was marching into Spain with Wellington. They were passing through a country where both armies had been marching to and fro and everything had been consumed and destroyed. They came one day to a large country house, and went in on the chance of finding something to eat still remaining. No one answered their knock so they went in and walked through the house until they came to a large room where they found seventeen people, twelve already dead, the rest dying of starvation. The dead had been neatly laid out with their hands folded on their breasts, and the living were sitting beside them patiently waiting for the end. Napier says that the English soldiers tried to save them with the small means at their command, and one man, though far gone, was anxious to eat and live; but the women were quite indifferent, they had already resigned themselves and were only waiting quietly and patiently for death.

I cannot, as I say, praise too highly or too often Don Carlos's courage and good temper and patience during this period which must have been so horrible for him. But there was something that did rather trouble us about his attitude to it all, and that was what I can only call a sort of good natured ferocity. When we were talking about the burning of houses in Malaga and we were explaining just which houses had been destroyed, it came out in a way that startled while it amused us.

'They burned that big book shop,' we said. 'You know, that one near the Café Ingles.' '*Bueno!*' said Don Carlos approvingly, 'We would have burnt that too.'

'And they burned the Conservative Press – what was it called, the *Union* Something-or-other – ?' '*Bueno!*' said Don Carlos with real enthusiasm this time, 'We would have burnt that too. Much too middle-of-the-road, not out-and-out enough! *Bueno! y que mas?*' 'Good! and what else – ?'

It was quite natural, I quite realised, that Don Carlos should sometimes dream of revenge, surrounded as he was by enemies. But his light-hearted references to the thousands they were going to shoot when they got to Malaga rather horrified us. We could not help feeling that it was just what *was* going to happen. This gay ferocity, and the increasing numbers of people and classes who became included in the term *canalla*, and were to be 'liquidated' sooner or later made us feel that on both sides Reason *had* been the first casualty: it depressed us a good deal. And Gerald who was both very humane and easily excited (and who could hardly stand the killing that was going on already) became extremely agitated sometimes (the situation was getting on all our nerves of course), and scenes were, with difficulty, avoided by tact and good feeling on both sides. But I must remark at this point that with so many reasons for being revengeful, Don Carlos was infinitely more reasonable, humane and understanding than so many of the foreign partisans of both sides I have encountered since, who fight their battles with such sound and fury in the Press of the world.

Finally as might have been expected everything came to a head. One morning there was an air raid on Malaga just at dawn, and Gerald and Enrique and I were watching it from the balcony. It was exciting at that distance with the crashing bombs, the anti-aircraft guns going off, the rattle of machine-guns and popping of revolvers, and the fighting planes from the field near us getting up belatedly. Suddenly after one bomb there was a tremendous flare-up near the sea, flames and black smoke began to pour up in a really appalling fire. A large heavy-oil dump had been hit.

We were horrified for we knew from often having passed the spot on the train that the heavy oil and petrol supplies, in very large quantities as Malaga is quite an important port, were concentrated in that one section near the sea, and one of the poor quarters of the city is built all around it. What would happen to that poor quarter if the large petrol tanks began to explode as seemed likely, frightened us to think of.

'Let's go up on the roof, perhaps we can see better there,' said Gerald much distressed. We went up on the roof and found Don Carlos and the boys already there. Don Carlos was almost dancing with excitement and pleasure over this Nationalist success. It was perfectly natural that he should be glad, I realised even then; but his happy mood clashed badly with our anxiety for the poor people in the suburbs of Malaga. And then Don Carlos, who was supposed to be in Malaga, had been seen in our house, delighting in the bombing, by people in the street, and had compromised us about as badly as possible and had made it infinitely more difficult to save him. Gerald was livid with exasperation and there was a painful scene while he explained bitterly the harm that had been done.

'I must go and find out what is happening,' he said as soon as we had calmed down and had some coffee, so we went down to the Village Square, but found as we expected that all buses and trains had been stopped by order: both the road and railroad track passed close to the fire. So Gerald borrowed a bicycle and went off. All the time the black smoke and red flames poured up unceasingly like an infernal fountain. In fact the fire burned without slackening for two days, and at night Malaga and the mountains behind it looked as if they had been painted in scarlet. The BBC that evening informed us that 'Malaga has probably been completely destroyed.' The flames had been seen for miles out to sea.

But what was extraordinary was that this terrific fire was entirely prevented from spreading. All the able-bodied men in Malaga turned out to pile wet sea-sand deeply over the underground petrol containers, some of the heavy oil which was in tanks above ground was run away into the sea; and the courage and enterprise of the Malagueñans saved their city from an appalling disaster.

Gerald came back a few hours later in a painful state of nervous horror. Even before he left we had heard that one bomb had not failed to find victims. There had always been a large gypsy encampment on the outskirts of Malaga and we had often enjoyed seeing them there, the children playing about in the dry earth, the mules eating a little dry fodder from the ground and the women nursing their babies or stirring the black pots which hung above the little fires. That morning a large bomb fell in the middle of the camp just when they were gathered together to eat their morning meal. Of the forty gypsies, only one, a terrified little girl, was left alive.

When they were telling us about it in the Square the villagers kept saying 'Oh! the poor *Hungaros*! What did they have to do with this war?' *Hungaros* means Hungarians (it is the name the Spaniards call foreign gypsies by) and some of the men added with their pathetic ignorance: 'Won't the Hungarian Consul do something about it?'

Gerald had arrived at the encampment before what was left of the gypsies had been cleared away. The ground was sodden with blood and covered with mangled, blackened bodies, and arms and legs and heads, torn off by the explosion and horribly littering the earth. Even when I passed the place a day or two later the earth was still dark with blood and the bodies of the poor dead mules still lay with their legs sticking straight up in the air and would have seemed absurdly like abandoned toys except for the odour of corruption beginning to taint the air.

Gerald, as I say, had come back from Malaga in a rather painfully nervous state. It was unfortunate that as he came up the street he caught the faint raucous sound of Seville broadcasting. Don Carlos was most unwisely listening to the Nationalist news; for it had been forbidden to listen in to the other side at that time, and of course our position was so delicate that we should have been particularly careful not to offend in any way. Gerald in his excited state felt outraged by the fact that Don Carlos appeared that day to be trying to make it as difficult as possible to save him. Then there was a further concealed cause of friction in the fact that the C—s did not seem to us to be as anxious to leave the country as we were to get them out. We did not like to insist all the time on the danger they were in: it seemed cruel to do so. And yet we could not help feeling that they did not properly appreciate how critical it all was. Afterwards we realised that we had done Don Carlos an injustice. He saw the danger even more clearly than we did. But his amazing courage made him able to treat the whole thing with apparent light-heartedness, since he believed that it was impossible for him to get out of the country, and probably fatal for him to try.

When Gerald came upstairs his mind full of horrible impressions, and heard the jubilant voice of the Seville broadcaster announcing their triumph, there was, as one might have expected, a painful scene.

It was natural that Don Carlos could not share our horror. He was sorry about the gypsies of course, but he could not help being pleased about the heavy-oil fire: it was an important Nationalist success. That kind of thing after all is the purpose of air raids. Whereas Gerald loathed air raids and did not want them to be successful anywhere. The wanton destruction of the poor gypsies, however unintentional, seemed particularly shocking: they had seemed so happily outside modern civilisation and its horrors.

That day as I was standing on the balcony watching the flame and smoke I heard high voices and saw a strange procession coming down the street. It was a small group of women, both young and old but all dark and handsome and dressed in the bright coloured cotton dresses with flounced skirts the Spanish gypsies wear. They were gypsies from the mountain who had heard of the tragedy and were coming down to Malaga to find out *who* had been killed – what mother or father, sister or brother, child or grandchild they had lost.

They came by with long strides and wild, strained faces, and with their torn dresses and long black hair loose and streaming in the wind they looked like frenzied Maenads; and at first I could hardly tell that the wild exalted look they wore was not an expression of religious ecstasy, but of an extremity of horror and fear.

Chapter 13

I HAVE SPOKEN of our friend the baker Juan. And at this point I should tell what happened to Juan. But I do not want to write about it, for my mind still avoids thinking of it even now as one might avoid touching an old but still sensitive scar. Perhaps I will come to it gradually by just talking about Juan.

Juan was a charming man, a bachelor of I suppose fifty or a little more, rather short but strong and muscular, and always smartly dressed in Sevillian style – snow-white shirt turned down around the neck without a collar but often with a white silk neckerchief, black trousers, made tight around the knees, a wide black sash bound tightly around the waist, and a black coat, thrown loosely over the shoulders in summer like a cape; the whole costume crowned with a wide stiff-brimmed hat of light grey felt. In fact to look at him, he might have been a breeder of bulls or at any rate a learned amateur of bullfighting. But really he had only a mild interest in bullfighting, his passion was for horses, and he always had one or two good ones. He really took more interest in his horses and his dogs and his farm than in his bakery, though he baked the best bread in the world, I truly believe, notable even among the wonderful breads of Andalucia, where to say *That village has bad bread* is almost as damning as to say *That village has a bad water* which removes it at once beyond the realm of civilised dwelling places.

I remember Maria taking a drink of water from the village well at Adra once when we visited that place. She had never left her mountains before and might well have been overcome by her first sight of the sea, falling in foam beneath her. However, all she said when she first viewed its endless blue waters was 'Can you wash clothes in it?' 'No,' we had to reply apologetically. 'Is it useful for irrigation?' she enquired again. 'No,' we were still obliged to reply. After which Maria lost interest in it, and turning her attention to the water she knew, went to taste a cupful from the big well in the square where some women were filling their pitchers. She just tasted it, and poured the rest of the water away.

'*This village,*' she said, '*has a bad water,*' and the women quailed before her, for, poor things, they knew that it was true.

Even now when I pick up the peculiar loaves, apparently made of an unattractive mixture of bleached sawdust and plaster-of-Paris, which we are forced to buy as bread in England for want of anything better, I daily regret Juan's bread. It is not that I 'want better bread than is made of wheat' as Cervantes says. I only want *bread* – and in England I am given something else. In Spain if I asked for bread I would get it. And Juan's bread was as honest as he was. It was *as good as bread*.

Juan, as I said, was a bachelor which is unusual in Spain, and he lived with a charming old mother of eighty-three. The village said that he had never married because he had had an unhappy love affair in his youth. He had fallen in love with a girl of another village, and she had loved him too, so the villagers said, but he was poor and her father was a wealthy man, and in the end she was married off to a richer suitor. But Juan never married, though he was an admirer of women, nor did he have a mistress. He lived with his old mother, and when he rode by in the village *fiestas* on his handsome horse, it was his niece who rode behind him dressed in her frilled Andalucian costume with flowers in her hair.

Juan used to come to see us from time to time and advise us about our fruit trees and crops, and we always both liked and admired him for he was a most attractive man. He was a conservative of a moderate sort and a devout Catholic; but he deplored the large neglected estates and the horrible poverty and lack of employment in Andalucia, and particularly the exploitation of the workers and the lack of security of the small farmers, who hired a bit of land and when they had improved it a little were often asked exorbitant rent on the score of the improvements they had made themselves, or saw it rented over their heads to someone with more means, as Juan told us with severe disapproval had been done many times in our village formerly, pointing out as we walked the orange trees and olive trees now tall and bearing, planted by the poor tenants who had been dispossessed.

'Something will have to be done!' he would say. It was a common saying in Spain. 'Hunger rules!'

Juan's family at one time had been much richer, and he was related to all sorts of people both rich and poor. His forefathers, I gathered, had ruined themselves in the common Spanish way, by having enormous families and dividing up their lands and money between such large numbers that in the end there was practically nothing left. I remember Juan taking us to see a fine house near the village once. 'My great-grandfather built that house for himself,' he remarked casually.

'But what a pity you haven't got it,' I said regretfully.

'Oh! I don't care much about houses,' Juan said indifferently. 'It's good land I like, a good irrigated piece like the one I have by the river, and then my horses and my dogs. In summer it's as much as I do if I go inside to see to the men in the bakery for a little while in the day and to sleep for a few hours at night. I'm out before it's daylight and after it's dark. Any four walls with a chimney in the corner would do for me if you left me my garden and my orchard and my vineyard.' He had the true Spanish passion for planting things and watching them grow.

Enrique couldn't even imagine anyone ever growing tired of being in a garden. He thought that with a garden like ours we all had happiness and amusement for our whole lives. Irrigating alone was a delightful occupation for two or three hours a day – I must say we used to love it too. We would watch with a sort of fascination the water beginning to bubble up in the middle of the flower beds just where Enrique wanted it from the pipes that ran underground from bed to bed; and then the watering of the fields, a carefully directed stream down the first furrow until that was full, then a few clever strokes with a hoe, a little dam built here, a new passage opened there, and the water streaming down to fill another furrow, led off sometimes by small canals to fill little moats around the fruit trees which stood in rows along the high orchard wall. 'Oh! there's always distraction in a garden!' as Enrique said, especially in a garden in Spain.

When we had visitors from England they had to spend their first evening watching the irrigating. It was as it were an initiation rite. But whether they ever caught the inner meaning of the Mystery of which Enrique was Initiate and Chief Priest, I do not know. Gerald and I were at least neophytes.

This Spanish feeling for land, for water, for sun, air, bread, olives, wine, all the simple and good 'gifts and creatures' as the prayer-book says is wonderfully expressed, I think, in a sixteenth-century folk-song – so Spanish, so unlike the folk-songs of other races. It is called '*Labradores de Castilla*'.

> Esta si que es siega de vida
> Esta si que es siega de flor.
> Hoy segadores de España
> Venid a ver a la Moraña
> Trigo blanco y sin Argaña
> Que de verlo es bendicion.

It is very difficult to translate it and catch any of the meaning and the feeling in it. Literally it says:

> This, this is the sowing of life
> This, this is the sowing of the flower.
> Today sowers of Spain
> Come to see at the Moraña
> Corn that is white and without tares,
> To see it is a benediction!

There is the voice of the true Spain, the lover of the land and of the flocks, of corn and wine and bread.

I write this here when I am speaking of Juan because he was such a true Spaniard, such a lover of the land, and a grower of corn and baker of bread. And when I think of these fundamental necessities of life as they are in Spain, and of the simplicity and happiness of the very act of living there, I cannot help remembering him – against my will, for I have so many painful thoughts connected with his memory now that I do not want to think of him at all. His ghost comes unbidden into my mind 'in his habit as he lived', and I see him walking about our garden with us on a bright Sunday morning, praising the beans, criticising the pruning of the oranges, but always kindly, while Enrique drank in eagerly praise, criticism and advice. I can see Juan's very smile and hear the very tone of his voice saying: 'You should buy some of the new American orange trees from the Agricultural Station. They are very dear, but they are worth it: there have never been oranges like that in Spain before! As to your vines – don't bother about them. I will get you cuttings of the best vines when your stock is ready for grafting. I have a friend –' In Spain one always had a friend, Juan was one of ours.

We could hardly believe it at first when we were told that Juan was 'wanted' by the extremists. But during the first week after the rising, an attempt was made to arrest him and several other poor men of the village and put them in Malaga prison under 'detentive arrest'. They were all middle-aged or elderly men in quite humble circumstances, and none of them I should imagine had had anything whatever to do with the risings. They were chiefly men who had been sergeants in the army or in the Civil Guard, and were supposed to have been cruel or repressive in their behaviour. Juan was much the most prosperous of them, and he was only the village baker with a few acres of land. It was not really for class reasons that people were murdered, in our village at any rate. It was for political hatreds or old *venganzas*. Juan had belonged to Gil Robles' Accion Catolica party, and had acted as electioneering agent and I suppose bought votes for it. That was his death sentence.

The village protested vigorously over this attack upon its rights, and won the first struggle over the fate of her *hijos*. It was agreed that they were to be allowed to stay in their homes, and that the village committee was to be responsible for them and to see that they did not try to escape. This was before Don Carlos and his family came to us, and we had the idea of having Juan stay in our house with the consent of the Committee, as being somewhat safer for him if the Terrorists made one of their night raids. But he preferred staying at home, as he said he had done nothing wrong and had nothing to be ashamed of, he was a member of a Centre party and not an extremist of any kind, he would stay in his own house.

At that time things were not so bad as they became later, and we hoped that he would be all right as he was popular in the village and had so many guarantees and safe-conducts from various sources. Later when we had the C— family with us it would have been impossible for us to have him. We were only just able to save Don Carlos by trading on our prestige as British subjects almost beyond what it would bear. I do not think it would have been possible for us to have kept Don Carlos even a week longer than we did. To take in Juan as well would have been very dangerous for them all.

Juan had some other English friends, fellow horse-lovers, who had a farm in the sierra and had remained on it, but he decided not to go to them when the question arose, because he said it would not be a good place to hide if *they* should come. But I think his decision not to go was partly due to unwillingness to leave his village. I remember how poor Maria and Pilar used to say at that time: 'Oh! Señora, if we were only all safe at home in *Our Village!*'

Don Carlos and Gerald and I were always inclined to think that Juan's best plan would probably be simply to go to Malaga and stay at one of the larger hotels in the middle of the town for a while. Except during one week when the terror was at its height these hotels were particularly safe places. They were locked and guarded at night, and while they were sometimes searched by militia, etc., during the day, it was not such searchers that Juan had to fear; his various safe-conducts would have protected him from anyone with the shadow of a legal authority, it was only the secret night murderers he had to dread. – But I do not know why I go over and over this when it is too late – I have even thought that if Juan had been a man of the active courage of Don Carlos he might have got safely over to the other side, crossing the sierra towards Algeçiras. It cannot have been very well guarded, and once he got out of the immediate district he would not have been recognised, and might have passed as a countryman travelling on business. He could have got passes and safe-conducts of all sorts. But the horrible change in everyone around him paralysed his energies, as a rabbit becomes paralysed at the approach of a snake.

For the change must have been dreadful to him. One by one his friends fell away, only his family, and they fearfully, shared his isolation. No one came near him, everyone avoided him. He sat in a little yard behind his house alone or with his one faithful friend, an almost half-witted man he had been kind to. There he sat through the long days, or lay through the longer nights in his room above. What a burden of suffering men and women have borne during this war!

When I was a child and used to read books about the Indian Mutiny certain names came to have for me a curiously sorrowful ring, a sad undertone seemed to sound when they were spoken –

Lucknow – Cawnpore. I have found since the Civil War began that certain names of Spanish cities have for me now this same sorrowful tone which sounds in my mind when I see them or hear them spoken – Badajos – Malaga – Toledo. Even Granada, whose charming name (which means pomegranate) used to call to my mind only the most delightful days spent among its bright squares and climbing streets, or hanging over the Alhambra wall gazing down fascinated on the city spread below while all the sounds of the south, the playing children, the calling women, the street cries, the cathedral bells, the crowing of the cocks floated up to us, sounds sadly now. It was our favourite city, and in the old days when we had been for months in the high wilds of the Sierra Nevada, and started off at last for an expedition to it, I used to understand Browning's peasant who keeps saying 'Oh! a day in the City Square is the greatest pleasure in life!' But now what a melancholy ring it seems to have – Granada – how sadly the syllables fall. And it is the same with all the Andalucian cities I have loved. Cordoba – Antequera – Almeria – they all have the same sorrowful sound.

When Don Carlos first arrived Juan came to visit him one day. He came a back way across fields because he said he would not return the Left Front salute if it were made to him, as it was almost sure to be, on the road from some passing lorry. Don Carlos whose courage was of a gayer kind did not sympathise with this stubborn attitude. 'I wish I had a duro for every time I've held up my arm,' he said. He had been caught in the trouble in Malaga when it began and had spent the evening saluting. I wanted to find out how close the watch kept on Juan was, and reconnoitring around the house, I found under the front windows trying to pick up a bit of the conversation in the *sala* a sort of spy-guard, a haggard old man sitting on a wheelbarrow in most unconvincing idleness. So I went out and talked to him, about the weather, about the bombing, about anything that came into my head, until he finally gave it up and went away. But a little later when I looked out he had returned again, so I sent Enrique out who invited him to come in and sit down in the kitchen if he was tired, which drove him away. But though the old spy amused us, he made us feel that the situation was worse than we had thought, and Juan did not repeat his visit which he realised was probably not well looked upon at a gathering of suspected persons.

Juan hardly ever went out after that. He sat all day in his house or in his backyard under the trees alone or with his poor friend, whose heart was better than his head. I remember a visit we paid him. We were talking as usual about his situation, and he spoke with a kind of horror of how his friends had fallen away, 'all except this one' he added, smiling at the faithful creature who sat beside him.

It was clear to us that the horror he felt was not simply at his own position. It was a sort of horror at the baseness and cowardice quite ordinarily decent kindly people can show when they feel themselves in danger, at the change that civil war can produce in hearts and minds.

When we got up to go that afternoon Juan looked at me as we said goodbye, and something in his whole nature called out to me so clearly that I felt as if he had spoken and said, 'What is it?' He answered me with a look which expressed more than I would have thought it possible to so express – something of real horror at the nature of the world as it was revealed to him, of a passionate all-consuming wish to wake at last from this nightmare he lived in – and then the connection between us was broken, and he only said hopelessly, '*Nada – nada –*' 'Nothing – nothing –'

We all wanted Juan to go to Malaga, we were sure that he would be safer there, where the Guardias de Asalto and Militia were strong enough to give real protection to people with safe-conducts. But fear made him irresolute, he could not decide. And then one night we came back from Malaga and heard that he had gone suddenly no one knew where. He had wanted to see us before he left, and unluckily we had been away. I do not know whether he wanted to come to us in his desperation or whether it was only to say goodbye. For some weeks we heard that he was in hiding somewhere, and we hoped that he might manage to hide successfully until things became safe again, or until the Nationalists took the city (an event which we all realised from the beginning was only a matter of time), as he had so many relatives of all classes and conditions – one for instance was an aviator at the local airfield. Many people did so manage to hide. The priest of our village, a young man who was generally liked as a good priest who was kind to the poor, got away to Malaga at the outbreak of trouble and hid successfully until the city was taken. He dressed as a workman, and, Don Carlos wrote us after the taking when he had returned, was bold enough even to go about the streets with a red handkerchief tied around his neck! His friend spread a story that he had escaped to Almeria where some of his family were known to live, which made him the less likely to be looked for. We hoped for a time that something like that would happen with Juan.

But the Terrorists grew impatient and announced that if they could not find Juan they would take his brother-in-law. It shows what a primitive race the Spaniards are in some ways that they were not much surprised or even much shocked at the idea of killing a member of his family in Juan's place. What did shock them was that they should talk of taking a brother-in-law – a brother, yes, they said, of course that would have been natural; but a brother-in-law is not really related. These were common tactics in the civil war, I am told, on both sides, for getting the man who was wanted. He almost always gave himself up to save someone else from suffering in his place: if he did not for some reason, at least they had a relative to kill or put in prison.

A few days later Maria came in and said angrily: 'They have killed Juan!'

It seemed that he had been hiding in a cave near a village up the valley; and some of his family had been secretly bringing him food at night. And he might have hidden there safely for a long time, but a friend gave him away, a friend who owed him money. Juan was shot. I hope he was killed instantly. After the first shock of horror at Maria's words I was conscious of a bitter relief. At least his long agony was over and Juan was safely dead.

Sometimes still in the night in those hours when there is nothing to distract us and the mind repeats its old troubles, I torment myself by going over and over the memories of that time – thinking that we might have saved Juan – that he might have saved himself – if he had acted differently.

Juan – Juan – my mind repeats, and the darkness answers *Nada – Nada –*

Chapter 14

THE SITUATION over Don Carlos became much worse after that fatal morning when he was seen on the roof. We had continual warnings about him. Finally the Village Committee told us that we would have to get rid of Don Carlos. They were being blamed for the situation, and could not protect him, nor be responsible for us with him in the house. They were very much worried. Gerald told them that he must keep Don Carlos a little longer whatever the consequences, but that he would try to make some other arrangements for him soon. Meanwhile he redoubled the efforts he was making to try to get them all safely out of the country.

Don Carlos had some very faint claim to be recognised as a Chilean citizen because he had once acted as Chilean Consul to the Argentine; but he had no papers whatever to show for it. The only thing which they fortunately did have were the children's nationality papers which showed that all except the youngest had been born in Chile and were Chilean citizens. Gerald made the most of these and enlisted the help of the Argentine Consulate which was acting for Chile. One day I remember he decided that Doña Maria Louisa and I had better go there and explain about Don Carlos's activities in Chile and the Argentine, and give them names of influential friends out there who might be able to vouch for them or help in some other way.

I remember it in a curious dreamlike way, for Gerald left us to wait there, as the Consul was out and he had other things to do. And we waited for a long, long time on a seat on a great stone stairway. All the time we sat there coffee and toast kept passing by on trays. And that odd procession of climbing meals, and the heat of the morning, and our anxiety have made a queer surrealist picture in my mind, so that I am not sure now what the place really was like. I do not think there *can* have been so many passing trays as I remember or that the steps can have been so huge and endless, like steps in Piranesi's dream drawings.

Finally the Consul came. He was a most charming man with one of those English names that have become famous in the Argentine. But he could not help us; we had no papers to show. He said that he would cable to Chile; but he could not give us much hope. Maria Louisa accepted his decision without a word of urging or complaint – in fact with her beautiful manners and her graciousness she seemed to be chiefly anxious to reassure him and make it easy for him to deal her this blow.

Meanwhile Gerald was 'multiplying himself' as the Spaniards say on the C—s' behalf. One day when he was in the Governor's office he asked them what he should do if the 'Uncontrollables' came. 'Shoot them!' they replied simply. But we did not really feel that shooting Terrorists was going to make our position any better. And as a matter of fact we never had the slightest intention of trying to use force ourselves, and had no arms of any kind except a life-preserver which Gerald had carried, but never used, on trench raids during the War, and an ancient fowling piece belonging to Enrique, which even he had doubts of firing.

Don Carlos heard that an old friend or acquaintance of his, Don Francisco D—, was on one of the Committees in Malaga, and suggested that Gerald should go to see him as he might be able to help. Unfortunately he was a Republican and consequently had not much influence. But we did go to see him and found him a most charming intelligent man and most willing to help us in any way that he could. I remember his daughter because she must have been typical of so many women at that time. She was in an extreme state of nervous agitation which she could not control. She was afraid for herself – afraid for her father – afraid of the Anarchists – afraid of the Nationalists. It was distressing to be with her. And her father with his Spanish stoicism was both distressed and annoyed by her lack of it.

He was a most reasonable and intelligent man, and was of course appalled by the whole situation; but he intended to do his duty as he saw it as long as it was possible for him to do so. He was one of those admirable and typically Spanish characters, whom the Spaniards themselves call 'noble' – and that is the best word I know for them. He most willingly agreed to help us by speaking for Don Carlos to the Central Committee. I wish I knew what has happened to him now. But perhaps it is just as well not to know. For when we said to Don Carlos that we hoped that he in his turn would be able to help Don Francisco when Malaga was taken, Don Carlos said that the Nationalists were sure to shoot him anyway.

On our way back from Don Francisco's house that day we met Sir Peter Chalmers Mitchell on the tram. There was nothing unusual about meeting him anywhere on the streets or trams or buses as he went a great deal into town to appeal to various committees for the large family of refugees he was sheltering, and also almost daily to visit the man of the family who was in prison, to find out how he was, and to take him what small comforts he was allowed to receive. But what was remarkable that day was the company we found him in. He was with a remarkably tough-looking young woman, dressed in blue overalls and wearing a revolver strapped to her belt. The contrast between this rather sinister person and the tall attractive figure of Sir Peter dressed as usual in immaculate summer clothes with fresh flowers in his buttonhole amused us very much for a minute and then filled us with some doubts especially as the pair did not seem to be on very good terms. So we drew Sir Peter aside and questioned him about his odd companion. He explained that she had made a declaration that his refugees owed her mother large sums of money for washing done for them in the past (as far as I can remember it), and had wanted to bring Doña Mercedes, the mother of the refugee family, before some tribunal about it. As Sir Peter was sure the accusation was false, but felt that it would be dangerous for Doña Mercedes to appear to deny it, he was going himself to try to argue the case before the tribunal (which he managed to do quite successfully, and even to get on fairly amicable terms with the denouncer, a poor creature from a miserable family, full of hate and spite against their former rich employers). We did not much like the sound of all this as it was explained to us over the rattling of the crowded tram, but as we could not do anything to help, we went on back to our own refugees.

An unexpected turn in our favour suddenly occurred when the Chilean Government asked the Madrid Government to allow the expatriation of whole families where some members of the family were of Chilean birth, as long as the Spanish members were not of military age. I do not know that the request was ever granted, but it allowed the Argentine Consul to give us a very dubious sounding paper, which described the C— family as having some Chilean members, and asked that they should be allowed to leave Spain and proceed to Chile where their affairs called them. We realised that this paper was neither passport, nationality papers, nor anything else with any legal authority; but the situation was getting so ominous that Don Carlos decided to try to get away with it. Gerald managed to get it stamped by the Governor's office and the 'Committee of Public Safety'. But would the paper prove sufficient when the time came for using it? And would we even get Don Carlos safely from our house to the boat?

However, the situation was getting so desperate that Don Carlos decided to try it and the very next morning when an American destroyer happened to be leaving. Then an anxious discussion began as to the safest way of getting to Malaga. And we all decided in the end that it would be best to go quite openly on the eight o'clock morning train, as that only stopped once at one little country station, whereas the cars and buses could be stopped anywhere along the road. The boys would have to go to their house to get a few clothes and get on the train at the little station which fortunately happened to be near it.

Maria Louisa and I afterwards confessed to each other that we did not sleep at all that last night: we were both so afraid that something would happen at the last minute. But the night was tranquil and the next morning we did exactly what we had planned. We all walked quite openly to the station saying good morning cheerfully to the people we passed as if we were going on a shopping expedition. I must say it was rather an alarming walk, and some of the people looked at Don Carlos very oddly; but nothing happened and we got on the train, and were profoundly relieved when it started, and went rattling along until it came to the next little station. What would happen there? I could not help remembering that it was there that they had taken off the two poor old priests to take them to prison. And would the boys be there? Yes, with a long breath of relief we saw them getting on, and felt the train starting. There was an even more anxious moment when we got to Malaga – would we be stopped at the barriers? But we showed our tickets and walked quietly through, then, as quickly as we could go without attracting attention, we carried Don Carlos off to the English Club, while Maria Louisa and the children went to her mother's house to say goodbye. We found that the destroyer did not leave until early in the afternoon, and we rashly took Don Carlos to the hotel where his sister and a nephew were staying and left him there for a little while to say goodbye. This we afterwards realised had been a perfectly mad thing to do, for we were told later that some of the Terrorists began to look for him in Malaga almost as soon as he left our house – word had somehow got to them. And that morning after we had gone three heavily armed strangers appeared at the door, and asked Maria if Don Carlos C— were there. Maria with her usual presence of mind and I daresay with a very severe manner which carried conviction said: 'You are too late. He has already left the country on his way to the Argentine.' I think this decided statement of Maria's with her stern manner, very effective in a country with a good many remnants of a matriarchal system like Andalucia, may well have saved Don Carlos's life. For they probably did not look for him in Malaga with the same conviction and perseverance they would otherwise have done. And the very boldness of his going to see his sister may well have turned out a wise move, for they would hardly have expected him to go there of all places.

Anyway all went well, and we were all sitting safely in the American Consulate long before the time for the destroyer to leave. Gerald had rushed out on some last minute task and I was holding the various papers of the family when the American Consul came up and looked at them.

'That Chilean paper is no good at all,' he said discouragingly. 'You'll never get them away with that,' he added, not realising that Don Carlos knew a certain amount of English. Don Carlos and I interchanged looks, glad that Maria Louisa and the children could not understand what he was saying.

Just then Gerald returned and we set off to the docks which were not far away. There we waited in a long shed in the really terrific afternoon heat, while the officials worked their way slowly through the long lines of refugees, Cubans and South Americans of all sorts, with a few Spaniards and one or two North Americans. The Chilean vice-consul, an intelligent and energetic young man who had been a great help to us all along had appeared, to be there in case anything went wrong. One of his most valuable qualities was that he had greater powers of conversation even than the Spaniards – and these powers were still to prove useful to us. For when Don Carlos's turn came, the officials refused to accept the paper of the Argentine Consulate, and said Don Carlos could not leave the country. Maria Louisa and I were in despair, and I suppose Don Carlos was too, though he did not show it. Gerald, however, was undaunted, he asked the Consul to hold the boat a little if necessary; and he and the Chilean vice-consul sprang into a taxi and rushed off to the Governor's office and the various committees again.

Gerald said afterwards that it was really the Vice-Consul who managed it. Not only did he have greater conversational powers than any Spaniard, he had twice the staying power, and all the energy of new continents. He talked them to a standstill, and if ever he flagged for a moment Gerald himself took up the strain. However it was done, just as Maria Louisa and I were really beginning to despair, the two appeared in triumph with the confirmatory document they wanted. This the embarkation authorities most unwillingly recognised, and we went as quickly as possible to the waiting ship's launch. As soon as we had hurriedly embraced and said goodbye, they stepped into the boat, and at a word from the Consul to the officer in charge, it pushed off from the shore, handled by some immaculate but extraordinarily rough-and-ready looking American sailors.

We stood waving on the dock. The long struggle was over: they were saved.

And the time has almost come for me to say goodbye too; though we did not leave for some time after the C—s went. Our position was never very pleasant again. Some people did not 'look at us very well' as the Spaniards put it. We were perfectly safe I think in spite of having saved a *Fascista*, but there was a certain amount of suspicion of us. People watched us doubtfully. They were not so sure of the innocence and simplicity of the English as they had been.

The day after the C—s got away is fixed in our memories as the day of our most startling war experience. We were sitting in the garden drinking coffee after lunch under the trees when a large silver grey aeroplane appeared overhead flying very low. We supposed that it was about to land at the airfield, and looked at it with interest as we had never seen any plane so large and modern looking from there before. Then suddenly there was a terrific explosion. A large bomb had fallen just outside our garden wall, spattering us with dirt. We rushed for the house; but there was another explosion close to us before we could reach it. We found the *sala* rapidly filling with our terrified neighbours who had been more suspicious than we had of the strange grey plane.

Then as we stood crowded together there was a perfect hail of bombs around us. The aviator appeared to us to be actually trying to hit the house. Explosion after explosion came on every side of us. One bomb crashed on the asphalt road in front, and the glass from the windows along the street came raining tinkling down. Two young girls had completely lost control of themselves and sobbed and shrieked in hysterics. The sound irritated and hurt me. I felt that I could either stand the repeated shocks of the bombs or the shrieks of the girls. The two together seemed unendurable. And the time seemed very long until it was all over.

Afterwards our neighbours counted the holes made by the explosions. They found that seventy bombs had fallen within two hundred yards of our house. We could not imagine why this violent attack had been made on this particular section of our poor village: all sorts of speculations were rife. But afterwards we were told that there had been an ammunition dump in the garden of a large white house near us for a short time, though the ammunition had actually all been removed before the raid. Of course the bombs used were quite small ones or the vibration caused by so many explosions in a small sector would have been serious, but even so the slight amount of damage done was remarkable. Only one bomb actually struck a house, that one fell on the roof of the school (which was empty of course) crashed through it – and did not go off. Two people were rather badly cut by flying glass and two goats and a donkey were killed. All the other bombs wasted themselves in digging holes in gardens or tearing up the streets.

Pilar, who had noticed that I seemed unusually nervous and irritated during the raid, sympathised with me over the hysterics of the girls. 'I could see that those girls shrieking like that made you nervous, Señora,' she said. It did not seem to occur to her that perhaps the bombs made me nervous too. This was flattering: but it was not true. For I did suffer from something almost like shell-shock for a time after that raid. But it was shell-shock of a curious kind; for its incidence was almost entirely confined to being in our garden. If I was out under the trees by the bed of zinnias the sight of a plane even on the distant horizon, or the sound of one, even though I knew it by its coughing to be one of the old local machines familiar to me even before the outbreak of war, would make me want to hurry into the house, and if I was alone I would yield to this urge to escape from the menace I felt in the air. Our garden which had seemed to me even during the war so safe and sheltered seemed to me after that raid a defenceless place open to attack from the Prince of the Air and all his evil Legions. I could not feel secure in it any more. In the house or the street or in Malaga I felt the same as ever, though just after that we had a number of disagreeable night raids. But in the garden I felt exposed, like a rabbit when there are hawks about. It had become the place where bombs fell suddenly out of the clear sky.

But before we left Spain we had been in so many air raids that I had come unconsciously to feel that all aeroplanes were potential murderers (a feeling with a good deal of justification) and when we first came back to England I could not really believe that the aeroplanes I saw were not coming to drop bombs. I could not help looking at them with a certain apprehension, expecting the first bomb to fall. Just as when I happened to see a burned house in England, I thought before I could stop myself, 'Why they've been burning houses here, too.'

Once in our village during the worst times, an old lady died; and we all began asking each other what had happened – surely they were not killing old ladies! And when we were told that she had died a natural death in her sleep, being extremely old, we were all strangely pleased. It was as if, like some savages, we had not known that people could die natural deaths.

Our leaving Spain in the end was a kind of accident. We decided to go to Gibraltar to get some money and find out what was happening, and then to return to Spain. Again the boat which was leaving happened to be an American destroyer. As we stood on its deck it looked as glittering and new as if it were immune to all the troubles of Europe. And we felt strange and out of place on it; for we could not leave behind our troubled thoughts about Spain – though Malaga looking lovely in the distance with its great cathedral and the Moorish castle on the hill, grew small and smaller until the destroyer, gathering speed, drew rapidly out to sea and they were gone.

Epilogue

THE SCENE OF MY EPILOGUE is laid in Lisbon on the morning of a late autumn day. After we left Spain we never returned after all. We stayed in Gibraltar for a time and then our affairs called us home. We tried to forget the war, but all the while it lay heavy and sore at the bottom of our minds – and lies there still, though now we can think of other things and almost forget it.

I think that, odd though it may seem, Gibraltar seemed to me almost a more unpleasant place to be in during the Civil War than Malaga itself. I remember the paeon into which Borrow breaks forth in *The Bible in Spain* when he crosses the frontier from the Spanish side, and comes upon 'noble' English faces – 'Protestant' too, I suppose, as that was Borrow's first requirement for nobility. Either I am less susceptible to nobility and Protestantism than Borrow was (which I am afraid is very likely!) or else the Rock has changed.

Before the war we used always to find it amusing with its cribbed and confined garrison life, full of the usual parties, quarrels, flirting, gossip and games. And those narrow shopping streets with their little booths whose Oriental shopkeepers lean out with dark clutching hands to draw you in and sell you papery silk kimonos embroidered with golden dragons for 7/6d. Those busy quarters with their dark foreign faces, wandering sailors of all nations and tourists straying about in the sun pricing the cheapjack wares, had a 'Somewhere East of Suez' effect which diverted us when we came fresh from village life in Spain.

Then there was the Rock Hotel, at the other extreme in every way.

In fact I used to feel on the occasions when someone invited us to it for a meal that one lunch there was almost enough to make a Communist of anyone. For some reason you felt concentrated there all the irresponsible stupidity of modern wealth. The sort of conversation you would hear from the tables around you, smug, self-complacent, secure in the power of unearned money – money which for the first time in history is not expected to carry any obligations with it, made me, for one, long for a cataclysm to shock these dulled creatures out of their stupid battening. I wished for it indeed as heartily as any of the Medieval Fathers of the Church would have done while they cursed them for their 'usury' and their refusal to undertake their part in the Commonwealth of God.

There were, however, guests at the Rock Hotel who were of a different sort. These were a number of Spaniards, mostly old ladies in black, who had left Spain after the Republic came in, or after the rising at Oviedo, and had been waiting in Gibraltar ever since for the revolution which was to come; and which finally more than justified their fears by coming in a more horrible, more devastating form than even these tremblers can have apprehended – though it came from a quarter they had not, I suppose, expected it from. Once the Civil War began of course, Gibraltar was absolutely crowded with refugees of every class and party, who carried on their hatreds comparatively harmlessly in neutral territory.

The Rock Hotel had always, as I say, produced a disagreeable effect, as luxury hotels are apt to do, especially when you come from a region where hunger is common. But during the Civil War Gibraltar as a whole made a most unpleasant impression. The poor refugees hated and feared, and occasionally broke out into disturbances; and their anxious, excited state made everyone feel troubled and insecure. Most of the civilians as well as the Army and Navy officers we met talked the most extraordinary nonsense about 'Reds' and 'Communists' and were bursting with incredible atrocity stories. For the real sufferings of the Spanish people of all classes they cared not a particle: it was not a subject which had the slightest interest for them. Perhaps it was natural enough: they were interested in riding and tennis, in swimming and bridge. What had the Spanish people or their sufferings to do with them?

Complete indifference we would not have minded very much, it is natural enough to be indifferent to the misfortunes of others; but what was particularly unpleasant in the attitude of the English at Gibraltar (and I might add of the Americans and most of the other foreigners one met), was that they combined this essential indifference and ignorance with the most violent prejudices and a perfect revelling in preposterous atrocity stories. They were generally not so much *for* the Nationalists (since they tried us extremely by depreciating the Spaniards as a race – an attitude only possible to those who have never known that extraordinary people) as *against* the 'Reds'. And it would have been amusing, if it had not been so discouraging to anyone who would like to think well of the human intelligence, to listen to some stalwart Englishman or Englishwoman holding forth about the 'Communists' and their extraordinary atrocities, then, sometimes, to see a look of doubt and hesitation come over their faces, and the uncertain question 'Which side *are* the Moors fighting on?' A remark occasionally varied, as it was by one Army woman I happened to be talking to, by violent indictments of those criminal 'Reds' who had brought over the wild Moors to attack their own country! If you pointed out that as a matter of fact it was the Nationalists who had brought over the Moors, it immediately became a wise and necessary measure. For Reason and Justice if not actually killed in time of war, are at least under detentive arrest.

While atrocities supposed to have been committed by the 'Reds' were naturally the favourite consumption, a number supposed to have been committed by the Nationalists were told with equal enjoyment. Even the crucified baby was crucified again (this time by the Nationalists), and seen by an English sentry from his post on the edge of Spanish territory. One very odd atrocity story about the Nationalists was told later on by some of the Italians who had been at the taking of Malaga. They said that the wounded militia in the hospitals had been intentionally so badly treated by the surgeons who were of secret Right sympathies that many were unnecessarily dying of slight wounds and many had been deliberately crippled by bad treatment. I should find this story hard to believe about surgeons anywhere: nothing would make me believe it about Spanish surgeons. For I have seen something of the medical profession in Spain, and I believe there is no country where it contains such devoted servants of humanity.

For those who talk as if Spain were the country of illiteracy, bull fights, massacres and atrocities, have forgotten, or have never known, that Spain (as well as being a country of a glorious history, a most beautiful language and a magnificent literature) is also the country of the saints. There is surely no other country where extraordinary, single-hearted, passionate goodness has occurred so often as in Spain. How many names come to the mind – Las Casas, the Dominican spending himself ceaselessly for the Indians, San Tomás de Villanueva and his devoted work for the prisoners and captives – and how many more. And if it does not now often find its outlet in the charitable works of the Church (though you will still find it there) as it did in times past, it is diverted into various lay activities, often into the care of the poor and suffering. But indeed you may find this single-hearted passion any-where in Spain, among the Sisters of Charity caring for the sick and poor, among the patient, starving mothers of hungry children, among the Anarchists – where you least look for it there starts the hare.

Not long before our time in Granada a saint lived there. He was a priest who worked among the poorest of the city. And I have often had the great pleasure of listening to stories about that exquisite character, lost to the world in love of God and devotion to men, from members of his own family, who told half laughing, half in wonder, these family legends of the saint, to whom money was something to give to the poor and food something to divide among the hungry.

And where but in Spain has there ever been a legal opinion like that of Father Francisco de Vittoria 'the father of International Law' and his colleagues at Salamanca, which made Dr Johnson say long afterwards 'with great emotion' as Boswell tells us: ' "I love the University of Salamanca, for when the question arose as to whether it were lawful to conquer the Indians the University of Salamanca gave it as their opinion that it was not lawful." '

But I must not begin to talk about the saints and the remarkable men of Spain or where would I stop!

It amused us to find that the only thing that really made people in Gibraltar feel that the Spanish War might have serious consequences after all was the possibility that the Calpe Hounds might not be able to hunt on the coast opposite Gibraltar that winter if the war kept up! – But General Franco was a *gentleman*, we were seriously told, and would no doubt manage to arrange it. I suppose he was expected to keep the war away from Algeçiras lest it inconvenience them. What General Franco and the other Spanish officers who found that this was the only preoccupation of most of the English officers and officials in connection with the war in Spain, can possibly have thought of English heads (not to mention English hearts) it is difficult to imagine.

But Gibraltar with its ignorant depreciation of the Spaniards, its empty fulminations, and its embarrassingly erotic lust for atrocities was really a most unpleasant place during the Civil War. And we left it with relief when our affairs at home called us back to England. We were on the boat going home when our ship stopped for half a day at Lisbon, and that is why I say that the scene of my Epilogue is laid there.

We had gone ashore to do some shopping and visit friends and Gerald had hurried off to see someone while I went to the office of Aero-Portuguesa to make some enquiries for a friend who was coming aboard. But it seemed that I had arrived at an awkward moment, and there was no one in the office who could speak more than a few words of anything but Portuguese which is the most incomprehensible of languages unless you speak it yourself, very rich and musical, but spoken, I always think, with a strangely Germanic accent, sounding rather like a Visigoth speaking late Latin.

I was waiting and had been waiting for some time when in my boredom I picked up a Portuguese journal, though I cannot read Portuguese very well either. It turned out to be a number glorifying the Portuguese forces, and was full of the sort of pictures we are always seeing in the news reels at the cinema, of sailors grouped on the decks of warships, naval guns being turned into position, soldiers playing games, or receiving their stew from camp kitchens and so forth. I was looking at the pictures without much interest and had in fact come to the advertisements of military tailors and naval outfitters, and was about to lay the paper down, when I turned over the last page, and saw something, which as George Fox says, 'struck at my life'.

It was a picture of a machine-gun, and under it were these words or others like them:

M— ARMS ARE THE BEST.
The M— Machine-Gun was chosen in open competition
in 1928 for the use of the Portuguese Army.
Enquiries of our Portuguese Agent Senhor —.
M— Arms Company.

It happened that I had never seen an advertisement of munitions manufacturers before. Coming fresh from the Civil War with my mind still overshadowed by its horrors I was affected by it in a way which perhaps it would be difficult for people still quiet and safe in England (for the present at any rate) to understand. In fact it would be hard for me to exaggerate the shock which that advertisement gave me. What is this world we live in? I thought. It seemed to me that I might well find on some other page of that sinister magazine another advertisement.

THE M— PISTOL.

The best weapon for
murder and assassination. Well tested.

Or (why not?):

NEW PREPARATION OF ARSENIC.

Impossible to detect.
Successfully used recent Brighton Murders.

For that would be the logical sequel to that advertisement of the M— Machine-Gun. It was selected after all for its efficiency and economy in killing people too. It is that well-tested machine-gun guaranteed to cut flesh and break bone better than any other, manufactured and sold to make a profit for certain factory owners and shareholders in foreign and neutral countries, who were here offering the pain and death of their fellow men for sale.

I put down the paper and pushed it away as if it were stinging me. I would not wait any longer for my thoughts troubled me and I felt unable to stay still, so I got up and went out. The day outside was radiant, the sunlight fell so brightly on bricks and stones that Lisbon might have been newly gilt for some golden festival: but I went sombrely through the bright streets. My mind was full of horrors, and I saw the mild faces around me as murderers – First Murderer: Second Murderer: Third Murderer: – like the cast in some Shakespearian Tragedy – and I myself as Fourth Murderer: a small but necessary part in the world's crime.

I walked down the bright street and the dark cloud went with me. But before I had gone very far I met something which I had liked so long that the sight of it pierced through the cloud and made me see how bright the world outside me was that day. What I saw was two of the tall fisherwomen who are so magnificent in Lisbon, great amazons with big baskets of fish on their heads striding splendidly along.

The Dictator had recently made a law that these women were to wear shoes, since their barefoot state both shocked propriety, and made visitors think that Portugal was a poor country. And the two women I met were observing the law and had bought some wretched cheap slippers, which they were however carrying in their hands to save wear and to be more comfortable. Just as they came up to me they happened to catch sight of a policeman in the distance and hurriedly stooped down to put on their slippers and observe the law as long as he was in sight. I could not help smiling at them, and they answered my smile with a half smile of complicity as they strode grandly on in spite of the shuffling slippers, their heads proudly holding up the heavy baskets of silver fish, like magnificent caryatids.

The cloud about my mind began to lighten. These were not Shakespearian murderers, but characters out of Dekker or Thomas Deloney. People are not always engaged in making war after all – they also cheat dictators and tease policemen. There are 'olives of endless age'. People dance and fly kites – I could see them sailing above the roofs of Lisbon. Even the Civil War, I thought, some day will be over: even its inevitable aftermath of terror and suffering will be forgotten at last. *Perhaps one day it will please us to remember even these things* when generations have passed away and the Civil War is a dim half-forgotten story of old tragedy – as legendary and far away and as shadowy and faint in its power to evoke pain as the War of the Seven against Thebes or the wars of Clusium and Rome.

As I stood looking after the tall striding fisherwomen I noticed the woollen head handkerchiefs they were wearing tied around their dark heads, and remembered that I had wanted to get one for a present for a friend, and perhaps one for myself as well; so I left the fashionable shopping streets and threaded my way through squares and alleys until I came to the poor quarter, the part of any city that I like best. There is a street of little drapers' shops I know, their cheap goods overflowing on to the sidewalks, and I walked along it until I came to the one which for some reason I liked the look of best, and went in. There were two fisherwomen inside already turning over the handkerchiefs: one of them was choosing one, but she could not make up her mind between the green one and the yellow. It is obviously a most serious choice when you have saved for months, even skimping yourself of the most necessary food to be able to buy one. It would be a tragedy to get the wrong one after all, to choose the yellow and be always regretting the green.

They were handsome women, tall and erect with fine heads; but with that gaunt austere look of the woman worker who has always worked too hard and never had quite enough to eat – it is a look I know so well in Spain and Portugal. At last the buyer chose her handkerchief, still hardly able to leave behind the rejected one: and with a sigh unwillingly put down the escudos to pay for it, and they went out. I watched them as they went and saw them stop in the doorway silhouetted against the sunlight in the street, the one who had bought the handkerchief (it was the yellow one) took it out of its wrapping to look at it once more and make sure before it was too late that she had not really preferred the green one after all. Then apparently satisfied, she wrapped it up again, and talking animatedly they hurried on.

I looked after them as they went away, and I knew that unless the Lord hardened my heart like Jonah's I could not be angry any more. It was impossible not to be reconciled to mankind for their sake – for the sake of these creature who starve themselves to buy a patch no bigger than a handkerchief of that beauty and colour the world denies them. Impossible not to love creatures who set their hearts on such little and innocent things. And I felt suddenly reconciled to the whole world – and even to myself, as I too began to turn over the soft handkerchiefs and could not decide between the red one and the grey.

Afterword

O F ALL THE FOREIGN eyewitness accounts of the Spanish Civil War, Gamel Woolsey's *Death's Other Kingdom* is one of the most moving and unusual. It is one of the few records of the war that is fuelled more by a love of Spain and its people than by any firm ideological standpoint. Woolsey was someone whose political position ran contrary to the *Left Review*'s famous assertion of 1937 that it was impossible for authors not to take sides on the issue of being for or against Franco and Fascism. But then, to her contemporaries, she would barely have been considered an author at all. By the time of her death in 1968, she seemed destined to go down in history merely as the wife of the writer and Hispanist Gerald Brenan.

In view of the sadness, frustrations and sheer bad luck that dogged her for much of her life, it is unsurprising that Woolsey looked back nostalgically to what she perceived as her idyllic early childhood spent on a plantation in South Carolina. Born there probably in 1895 (a fear of ageing apparently made her put forward this date to 1899), she was descended on her mother's side from an old and distinguished South Carolina family. Her mother had been a celebrated beauty who, when only nineteen, had married a New York widower over twice her age. Woolsey had an elder sister with whom she was never close, and three half-brothers who thought of her as a strange child whom they could never fully understand. A dreamer, as well as a precocious reader, she immersed herself in fairytales and ancient myths, and even abandoned her real name of

Elizabeth in favour of the more poetic Gamel, after the Norwegian word for 'old'.

Melancholy and guilt became integral to her personality when she was still in her teens. When she was fifteen her father died, and, two years later, she fell in love with a childhood friend who committed suicide on discovering his homosexuality. Shortly afterwards her mother started drinking heavily, so much so that the horrified Gamel would not touch a drop of alcohol for many years afterwards. On top of all this, aged twenty, she was diagnosed with tuberculosis, and had to spend a year in a Charleston sanatorium, where she had half a lung removed. On leaving, she ran away to New York, married a womanising New Zealand journalist, and entertained vague hopes of becoming an actress or a writer.

By 1926 she had separated from her husband after miscarrying (or perhaps even aborting) the child she had been expecting by him. As with the protagonist of her romantic novel based on her New York years and their aftermath, *One Way of Love*, she was 'waiting for her knight on horseback to appear'. In 1927 such a person materialised in the unlikely figure of Llewelyn Powys, the youngest of that precious literary trio, the Powys brothers. A forty-three-year-old fellow tuberculosis sufferer, Llewelyn was married to his literary editor Alyse Gregory, a woman who believed strongly in feminine and personal independence. Alyse's beliefs would be put firmly to the test after her husband fell passionately in love with Gamel, who obsessed him with her dreamy, enigmatic personality, not to mention her 'large lovely breasts with the exquisite hazelnut nipples'. In the late spring of 1928 Llewelyn received the news, delightful to him, but devastating to Alyse, that he had made Gamel pregnant. But, once again, Gamel was to lose her child. Following an accident in a taxi, and in the light of her tubercular history, her doctor insisted on her having an abortion.

Miraculously, Llewlyn's marriage to Alyse survived all this, as did his relationship with Gamel, and Gamel's close friendship with the

Gamel at Yegen in 1933

lesbian-inclined Alyse. When, in May 1928, Llewelyn and Alyse moved back to England and to the Powys heartland of the Dorset hills, Gamel followed suit, and took up lodgings twelve minutes' walk away from her lover. She was pregnant again by July, though once again she was impelled to have an abortion. Alyse, meanwhile, contemplated suicide.

By July 1930, Gamel was desperately trying to find a way out of this emotional impasse. It was now that an aspiring writer turned up in Dorset, no less desperate to find himself a wife, and armed with a letter of introduction to one of the Powyses.

This man, Gerald Brenan, had been living on his own for much of the previous decade in the remote Andalucian village of Yegen. There he had immersed himself in the study of Spanish history and culture, while battling with the sexual hang-ups induced by a repressive English middle-class background. As open in his discussion of his intimate life as Woolsey was closed, Brenan had little inhibitions about telling his friends (and later his readers) the minutest details of his affairs. His great passion during the Yegen years was with Lytton Strachey's partner Dora Carrington, with whom Brenan had a long, masochistic and largely epistolary relationship. In the two years immediately prior to his meeting with Gamel, Brenan had attempted a definitive break with Carrington and had returned to Spain to carry out an affair with fifteen-year-old Juliana, a Yegen girl with a healthy appetite for sex.

As with other British writers, Spain had a liberating effect on Brenan. His intensive love-making with Juliana, though inducing long periods of physical lethargy and wreaking havoc with a projected biography of Saint Teresa of Avila, made him finally overcome his habitual impotence. Unfortunately, this breakthrough also had the effect of making Juliana pregnant. Responding to this situation like some benevolent feudal landlord of old, Brenan placated Juliana with the offer of money and the promise of eventually looking after the child.

Faced now with the imminent prospect of becoming a single father, Brenan's search for someone with whom he could truly share his life became more urgent than ever. Within a month he had set eyes on a woman whom he immediately sensed would fulfil such a role. Brenan first saw Gamel standing 'mysteriously' beside a haystack. He was reminded of a grandmother of his, and was also forcibly struck by her beauty, which he would later try and convey in his at times disarmingly honest autobiography *Personal Record*. Among his first impressions of her were of someone with a 'fine bone structure', a transparent complexion of a kind 'that one sometimes finds in consumptive people', and 'calm grey eyes' that looked out 'gravely' from behind thick, 'blue black hair'. Several months later, when Brenan nervously introduced her to his parents, she surprised Brenan's father by displaying a degree of refinement he did not associate with 'a new, raw country like America'. 'Centuries of breeding,' the father openly declared in front of her, 'must have gone to the making of that mouth and chin'. It is unlikely that he would have made such a comment about the dumpy and frizzy-haired Juliana.

Yet for all Gamel's apparent suitability as a wife, it soon became obvious that there were enormous differences between them. There was, as Brenan realised, an almost schizophrenic quality to Gamel's personality. The ironic wit and lively intelligence she displayed one moment could be replaced the next by the apathy and silence that announced her withdrawal into her own private world. What was worse, she was still very much in love with Llewelyn.

On becoming engaged to Brenan, after knowing him only a few weeks, Gamel told Llewelyn that this new development would in no way effect their own relationship. 'I am very fond of Gerald,' she later wrote to him, 'but it has nothing to do with what I feel for you. We meet in some part of the mind where other people never come.' To the understandably jealous Brenan she announced that the love between her and the selfishly and childishly possessive Llewelyn 'transcended all other loves' and that it had 'something supernatural about it'.

Gamel and Brenan, in the course of the nine-month 'honeymoon' on which they embarked in the autumn of 1930 (they would not officially marry until 1947), succeeded in overcoming numerous traumas, ranging from Gamel's spell in a Norfolk sanatorium to a return of Gerald's impotence. Brenan discovered in Gamel 'the perfect travelling companion', and also assumed with relish a new role as her protector, finding in her a need to be protected greater than in anyone he had ever known. None the less their marriage was clearly not going to be one based on passion ('Llewelyn had seen to that'). 'There was always something wanting in our deeper feelings for one another,' confided Brenan in *Personal Record*. Woolsey, in a letter to Llewelyn of 1936, put the same sentiment across rather more strongly: 'Gerald has never got in touch with most of my mind at all, or even wanted to, or would be interested if he did. And I'm sure large tracts of his mind are equally sealed to me.'

For Gamel in particular the post-honeymoon return to England in the summer of 1931 must have been especially difficult. Quite apart from having to cope with renewed proximity to the emotionally manipulative Llewelyn, she must have been painfully conscious of the comments made about her by Brenan's hypercritical Bloomsbury friends. Everyone, for instance, found her clothes sense to be disastrous, while Carrington and Strachey ascribed to her the ultimate Bloomsbury sin of being a bore.

Compensations and frustrations were provided by her first taste of English literary life. Brenan, who had yet to bring out a single book, and had been struggling for ages with a novel of his own, must have become secretly envious when, in 1931, a volume of Gamel's poems (of which he had never thought much) was published under the title *Middle Earth*, and a deal was arranged with Gollancz to publish *One Way of Love*. However, as was so typical of Gamel's thwarted life,

Gollancz, after having set the book in print, relented on the deal in February of the following year. They were worried about being prosecuted for obscenity, which was ironic given that one of Gamel's half-brothers was a judge famous for defending first Marie Stopes and then James Joyce against such charges.

The failure to publish *One Way of Love* was overshadowed by other crises that year, beginning with the suicide of Carrington in January, and proceeding in August to a severe cancer scare involving Gamel having a lump removed from her breast. Brenan, who had still not seen his illegitimate child by Juliana (a daughter called Miranda), thought that the moment had now come to introduce Gamel to Spain and to Yegen.

Gamel was instantly overwhelmed by the beauty of Andalucia, and appears to have been unaware of rumours that Juliana was trying to win Brenan back with the use of love philtres. Gamel's enthusiasm for Spain increased further when they went back to the country early in 1935, to set up home with Miranda in the rambling old house near Malaga that is the setting for *Death's Other Kingdom*. Memories came back to her of her childhood, and she wrote to Llewelyn that the place 'was beautiful and abandoned and romantic like an old plantation house where ruined people have been living for generations.' She would never fully master the Spanish language, and she had particular difficulties at first understanding even the Andalucian utterances of Miranda. But she had somehow discovered in Spain her spiritual home.

It was not the best time to have done so. Intimations of some impending national tragedy were felt by Brenan as early as the spring of 1935. But Brenan and Gamel, like so many other expatriates in southern Spain, pretended to themselves that nothing serious would really happen. An excellent portrayal of the Malaga they knew immediately before and during the Civil War was given by their acquaintance Chalmers Mitchell in his book *My House in Malaga* (1937). Chalmers Mitchell, a former director of London Zoo, was described by Gamel in a letter to Llewellyn as a 'delightful old man', and features in both *Death's Other Kingdom* and *Personal Record* as an eccentric dandy risking the wrath of the Republicans by dressing, in Brenan's words, 'in an immaculate white alpaca suit, complete with a bow tie'. He had come to Malaga in the 1930s in the expectation of a peaceful retirement, and, right up to the very outbreak of the war, had little inkling that this was not going to be possible.

The months leading up to the Civil War appear from Chalmers Mitchell's description to have been an almost blissful period in Malaga, blessed by a 'particularly beautiful Spring', and with the burgeoning British community entertaining itself with 'much bridge at the club; golf on a rather inefficient but beautiful course recently opened, motoring into the neighbourhood, walks, and mutual visits for luncheons or dinners or teas.' More visitors than ever were contemplating buying or building villas in the area, and the British Club in Malaga, soon to be deserted, was planning an enormous extension for the summer.

When, on the hot and sunny afternoon of 18 July, gun shots rang out and the horizon became obscured by fires, there was almost a sense of disbelief among the hundreds of British residents and visitors, most of whom (including the young Laurie Lee at nearby Almuñecar) soon left the country. The anger and indignation that so many of them displayed on their departure shocked Brenan and Gamel and might have strengthened their own resolve to stay on in Spain as long as possible. Brenan later admitted that he had felt completely ashamed at being British. Both he and Gamel, faced with a national crisis, became aware of how petty their own problems were in comparison with the fate of the Spaniards. And, like Chalmers Mitchell, who also remained in Malaga, they showed a concern for people that transcended their political sympathies. All three of them, though broadly supporting the besieged Republican government, were willing to compromise themselves by sheltering in their houses prominent right-wing families.

Gerald Brenan at Churriana in 1936

Gamel, in a letter to Llewelyn describing the chaotic situation of this time, noted that 'Gerald, I need hardly say, is enjoying himself hugely.' She herself had an abhorrence of war, and memorably coined the phrase 'pornography of violence' to describe the relish and exaggeration with which atrocities were often reported. Yet she herself was candidly to admit to the thrill of living life at such a heightened intensity. War certainly brought out the best of her, not just as a person, but also as a writer. It released her from her morbid and self-indulgent introspection, and gave her a much-needed sense of purpose as well as the concern for common humanity that is so striking a characteristic of *Death's Other Kingdom*.

Death's Other Kingdom was written after their eventual return to Britain, at the same time as Brenan was maniacally working on his brilliantly lucid exposition of the war, *The Spanish Labyrinth*. While Brenan grappled with the big issues, Gamel dwelt on the domestic minutiae, such as in her book's funny and touching last page, when a couple of impoverished fisherwomen heatedly debate which colour handkerchief they should buy.

Characteristically for Gamel, circumstances conspired to prevent the book from enjoying the degree of success it deserved. After finally signing a contract with Longmans in April 1939, Gamel was told that publication would be delayed until the autumn of that year, by which time, as she wrote to Llewelyn, 'I think we may all be in Death's Other Kingdom.' Another matter of concern was the choice of author to write the introduction. The publishers approached the poet Edward Blunden (the only author apart from Evelyn Waugh to have taken Franco's side in the *Left Review*'s symposium on the war). Fortunately he declined the offer, much to the relief of Gamel, who thought him 'a *very* bad writer'. She herself favoured Bertrand Russell, an ardent male admirer of hers; but he was rejected by the publishers on the grounds of being 'too political'. There was talk for a while of Siegfried Sassoon; but finally the task fell to Llewelyn's brother John Cowper Powys.

Gamel expressed her approval, though it is difficult to imagine that she would have liked the pompous and patronising text he ended up writing. His fitting praise for her personal and intimate way of looking at the war was completely diminished by his saying that hers were qualities 'permitted only to women – that is to women when they're not maddened by the hysteria of sex.' Furthermore his conclusion that the book was essentially 'a tender and wistful threnody over "Old Spain" by a daughter of the "Old South" ' would have misled readers into thinking that the work was yet another contribution to the gushing, romantic literature on the country.

The book received a handful of enthusiastic notices, and was praised by the *Times Literary Supplement* as 'moving and beautiful'. But any satisfaction she might have derived from this would have been muted by the almost simultaneous death of Llewelyn and arrival of another and far greater war, in the course of which her subtle and understated book would soon be forgotten. Brenan would be far luckier with the timing and reception of *The Spanish Labyrinth*, which appeared in 1943, received massive coverage and immediately established its author as the foremost Hispanist of his day.

Gamel and Brenan returned to Spain soon after the Second World War, the latter to research his travelogue *The Face of Spain*, which portrays the country at the height of its 'years of hunger'. With nervous anticipation they went back to their house at Churriana, and were relieved to find the place almost as Gamel had so evocatively described it in *Death's Other Kingdom*, and with the same memorable cast of characters. The reunion with those whom they had left behind was filled with emotion, as was their renewed contact with their garden, which appeared more luxuriant and exotic than ever. When they set off again on their travels, they felt, according to Brenan, as Adam and Eve must have done on the point of being expelled from paradise. But they would be back for good five years later, this time to witness Churriana being gradually enveloped by the urban sprawl that came to be known as the Costa del Sol. Brenan was unperturbed by this, and indeed relished the new influx to the coast of young and liberated women. To Gamel, however, this spoiling of their surroundings could only have contributed to the growing misery of her last years.

Childless, and insufficiently recognised as a writer, Gamel came to think of her life as a failure. On settling back in Churriana, she moved into a separate bedroom to her husband, dyed her hair black, and became absorbed by the reading of science fiction, finding in it metaphors for her own strange and solitary existence. She also dwelt pathetically on the past. 'Oh Gamelismus!' recorded Brenan's friend Frances Partridge on a visit to Churriana in 1962, 'I did laugh inwardly yesterday at the way she brought out faded passport photographs of Powyses, or others of houses of no possible significance in Charleston and views in the mystic South, hoping by these totem objects to prove that she too had a significant past among the illustrious.'

Gamel persisted sporadically in her literary activities, and, despite the limitations in her understanding of Spanish, revealed herself as an outstanding translator in *The Spendthrifts*, which introduced the English-speaking world to Pérez Galdos's dazzlingly original novel *La de Bringas*. However, it was as a poet that she wanted above all to be recognised; and this ambition was shattered when T. S. Eliot, whom she greatly admired, rejected her poems for publication. She succumbed to cancer shortly afterwards.

Brenan, overcome with pity at seeing Gamel dying so unfulfilled, made efforts after her death in 1968 to keep her memory alive. He privately printed several volumes of her verse, and tried to persuade publishers to reissue *Death's Other Kingdom*. This last task was eventually undertaken by the feminist imprint Virago, who also saw at last to the publication of the novel *One Way of Love*. Though the novel achieved a modest commercial and critical success, it is only

Death's Other Kingdom that is likely to endure, and not simply as a poignant account of an Andalucian village during the Civil War. Re-reading the book today, one is struck by how pertinent it remains as a commentary on war in general, and on war's impact on the lives of those ordinary human beings whom the rhetoric of politics and ideology never reaches.

MICHAEL JACOBS
Spain, 2004

ELAND

61 Exmouth Market, London EC1R 4QL
Tel: 020 7833 0762   Fax: 020 7833 4434
Email: info@travelbooks.co.uk

Eland was started in 1982 to revive great travel books that had fallen out of print. Although the list has diversified into biography and fiction, it is united by a quest for the defining spirit of place. These are books for travellers, readers who aspire to explore the world but who are also content to travel in their mind. Eland books open out our understanding of other cultures, interpret the unknown, reveal different environments as well as celebrating the humour and occasional horrors of travel.

All our books are printed on fine, pliable, cream-coloured paper. Most are still gathered in sections by our printer and sewn as well as glued, almost unheard of for a paperback book these days. This gives larger margins in the gutter, as well as making the books stronger.

We take immense trouble to select only the most readable books and therefore many readers collect the entire series. If you haven't liked an Eland title, please send it back to us saying why you disliked it and we will refund the purchase price.

You will find a very brief description of all our books on the following pages. Extracts from each and every one of them can be read on our website, at www.travelbooks.co.uk. If you would like a free copy of our detailed catalogue, please write to us at the above address.

ELAND

'One of the very best travel lists' WILLIAM DALRYMPLE

Memoirs of a Bengal Civilian
JOHN BEAMES
Sketches of nineteenth-century India painted with the richness of Dickens

A Visit to Don Otavio
SYBILLE BEDFORD
The hell of travel and the Eden of arrival in post-war Mexico

Journey into the Mind's Eye
LESLEY BLANCH
An obsessive love affair with Russia and one particular Russian

The Devil Drives
FAWN BRODIE
Biography of Sir Richard Burton, explorer, linguist and pornographer

Turkish Letters
OGIER DE BUSBECQ
Eyewitness history at its best: Istanbul during the reign of Suleyman the Magnificent

My Early Life
WINSTON CHURCHILL
From North-West Frontier to Boer War by the age of twenty-five

A Square of Sky
JANINA DAVID
A Jewish childhood in the Warsaw ghetto and hiding from the Nazis

Chantemesle
ROBIN FEDDEN
A lyrical evocation of childhood in Normandy

Viva Mexico!
CHARLES FLANDRAU
A journey among the Mexican people

Travels with Myself and Another
MARTHA GELLHORN
Five journeys from hell by a great war-correspondent

The Weather in Africa
MARTHA GELLHORN
Three novellas set among the white settlers of East Africa

Walled Gardens
ANNABEL GOFF
An Anglo-Irish childhood

Africa Dances
GEOFFREY GORER
The magic of indigenous culture and the banality of colonisation

Cinema Eden
JUAN GOYTISOLO
Essays from the Muslim Mediterranean

A State of Fear
ANDREW GRAHAM-YOOLL
A journalist witnesses Argentina's nightmare in the 1970s

Warriors
GERALD HANLEY
Life and death among the Somalis

Morocco That Was
WALTER HARRIS
All the cruelty, fascination and humour of a pre-modern kingdom

Far Away and Long Ago
W. H. HUDSON
A childhood in Argentina

Holding On
MERVYN JONES
One family and one street in London's East End: 1880–1960

The Tuareg
JEREMY KEENAN
The definitive academic study of these proud desert people

Three Came Home
AGNES KEITH
A mother's ordeal in a Japanese prison camp

Peking Story
DAVID KIDD
The ruin of an ancient Mandarin family under the new Communist order

Scum of the Earth
ARTHUR KOESTLER
Koestler's personal experience of France in World War II

A Dragon Apparent
NORMAN LEWIS
Cambodia, Laos and Vietnam on the eve of war

Golden Earth
NORMAN LEWIS
Travels in Burma

The Honoured Society
NORMAN LEWIS
Sicily, her people and the Mafia within

Naples '44
NORMAN LEWIS
Post-war Naples and an intelligence officer's love of Italy's gift for life

A View of the World
NORMAN LEWIS
Collected writings by the great English travel writer

An Indian Attachment
SARAH LLOYD
Life and love in a remote Indian village